D0467485

Facing the Lion

Facing the Lion

Growing Up Maasai on the African Savanna

by Joseph Lemasolai Lekuton
with Herman Viola

NATIONAL GEOGRAPHIC

WASHINGTON, D.C.

Published by the National Geographic Society.

Book design by Cindy Min
The body text of the book is set in Spectrum MT.
The display text is set in Senator.

The verses that introduce each chapter
come from a traditional Ariaal warrior song.

Library of Congress Cataloging-in-Publication Data

Lekuton, Joseph.
Facing the lion : growing up Maasai on the African savanna / by Joseph
Lekuton with Herman J. Viola.
p. cm.
Summary: A member of the Maasai people describes his life as he grew up in a
northern Kenya village and traveled to America to attend college.
ISBN 0-7922-5125-3 (Hardcover)
ISBN 978-0-7922-7297-7 (Softcover)
1. Lekuton, Joseph—Juvenile literature. 2. Masai (African
people)—Kenya—Biography—Juvenile literature. 3. Masai (African
people)—Kenya—Social life and customs—Juvenile literature. [1.
Lekuton, Joseph. 2. Masai (African people)—Biography. 3. Masai (African
people)—Kenya—Social life and customs. 4. Blacks—Kenya—Biography.]
I. Viola, Herman J. II. Title.
DT433.545.M33L45 2003
967.62'004965—dc21
2003000750

Printed in the United States of America
09/WOR/5

Dedication

These words are dedicated to my mother, Nkasiko.
Although unable to read or write, she gave me a priceless
education. And to my mothers in America, Bea, Ricki,
Jackie, Anne, Betty, and Kathleen, who reflected and
reinforced my mother's philosophy of life.
And to all the nomadic boys and girls
who have similar stories.
My story is theirs;
I just had the chance to tell mine.

Table of Contents

Chapter 1   A Lion Hunt   9

Chapter 2   The Proud One   19

Chapter 3   Cows   25

Chapter 4   The Pinching Man   35

Chapter 5   School   43

Chapter 6   Herdsman   57

Chapter 7   Initiation   65

Chapter 8   Kabarak   75

Chapter 9   Soccer   85

Chapter 10   America   93

Chapter 11   A Warrior in Two Worlds   105

Afterword   111

Chapter One
A Lion Hunt

My sweet mother,
Don't call me a baby.
I stopped being a baby when I was initiated.

I'M GOING TO TELL you the lion story.

Where I live in northern Kenya, the lion is a symbol of bravery and pride. Lions have a special presence. If you kill a lion, you are respected by everyone. Other warriors even make up songs about how brave you are. So it is every warrior's dream to kill a lion at one point or another. Growing up, I'd had a lot of interaction with wild animals—elephants, rhinos, cape buffalo, hyenas. But at the time of this story—when I was about 14—I'd never come face-to-face with a lion, ever. I'd heard stories from all the young warriors who told me, "Wow, you know yesterday we chased this lion——" bragging about it. And I always said, "Big deal." What's the big deal about a lion? It's just an animal. If I can defend myself against elephants or rhinos, I thought, why not a lion?

I WAS JUST BACK from school for vacation. It was December, and there was enough rain. It was green and beautiful everywhere. The cows were giving plenty of milk. In order to get them away from ticks, the cattle had been taken down to the lowlands. There's good grass there, though it's drier than in the high country, with some rocks here and there. There are no ticks, so you don't have to worry about the health of the cattle, but the area is known for its fierce lions. They roam freely there, as if they own the land.

I spent two days in the village with my mom, then my brother Ngoliong came home to have his hair braided and asked me to go to the cattle camp along with an elder who was on his way there. I'd say the cattle camp was 18 to 24 miles away, depending on the route, through some rocky areas and a lot of shrubs. My spear was broken, so I left it at home. I carried a small stick and a small club. I wore my *nanga,* which is a red cloth, tied around my waist.

It took us all day to get there, but at sunset we

were walking through the gap in the acacia-branch fence that surrounded our camp. There were several cattle camps scattered over a five-mile radius. At night we could see fires in the distance, so we knew that we were not alone. As soon as we got there my brother Lmatarion told us that two lions had been terrorizing the camps. But lions are smart. Like thieves, they go somewhere, they look, they take, but they don't go back to the same place again.

Well, that was our unlucky day. That evening when the cows got back from grazing, we had a lot of milk to drink, so we were well fed. We sat together around the fire and sang songs—songs about our girlfriends, bravery songs. We swapped stories, and I told stories about school. The others were always curious to understand school. There were four families in the camp, but most of the older warriors were back at the village seeing their girlfriends and getting their hair braided. So there were only three experienced warriors who could fight a lion, plus the one elder who had come down with me. The rest of us were younger.

We went to bed around 11:30 or 12. We all slept out under the stars in the cattle camp—no bed, just a cowhide spread on bare soil. And at night it gets cold in those desert areas. For a cover I used the nanga that I had worn during the day. The piece of cloth barely covered my body, and I kept trying to make it longer and pull it close around me, but it wouldn't stretch. I curled myself underneath it trying to stay warm.

Everything was silent. The sky was clear. There was no sign of clouds. The fire was just out. The stars were like millions of diamonds in the sky. One by one everybody fell asleep. Although I was tired, I was the last to sleep. I was so excited about taking the cows out the following morning.

During the middle of the night, I woke to this huge sound—like rain, but not really like rain. I looked up. The starlight was gone, clouds were everywhere, and there was a drizzle falling. But that wasn't the sound. The sound was all of the cows starting to pee. All of them, in every direction. And that is the sign of a lion. A hyena doesn't make them do that. An elephant doesn't make them do that. A person doesn't. Only the lion. We knew right away that a lion was about to attack us.

The other warriors started making a lot of noise, and I got up with them, but I couldn't find my shoes. I'd taken them off before I went to sleep, and now it was pitch black. Some warriors, when they know there's danger, sleep with their shoes in their hands and their spears right next to them. But I couldn't find my shoes, and I didn't even have a spear. Then the lion made just one noise: *bhwuuuu!* One huge roar. We started running toward the noise. Right then we heard a cow making a rasping, guttural sound, and we knew that the lion had her by the throat.

Cows were everywhere. They ran into one another and into us, too. We could hear noises from all directions—people shouting, cows running—but we couldn't see a thing. My brother heard the lion right next to him and threw his spear. He missed the lion— and lucky for the rest of us, he missed us, too. Eventually, we began to get used to the darkness, but it was still difficult to tell a lion from a cow. My brother was the first to arrive where the cow had been killed.

The way we figured it was this: Two lions had attacked the camp. Lions are very intelligent. They had split up. One had stayed at the southern end of the camp where we were sleeping, while the other had gone to the northern end. The wind was blowing from south to north. The cows smelled the lion at the southern end and stampeded to the north—toward the other waiting lion.

When I asked my brother, "Hey, what's going on?" he said, "The lion killed Ngoneya." Ngoneya was my mother's favorite cow and Ngoneya's family was the best one in the herd. My mother depended on her to produce more milk than any other cow. She loved Ngoneya, really. At night she would get up to pet her.

I was very angry. I said, "I wish to see this lion right now. He's going to see a man he's never seen before."

Just as we were talking, a second death cry came from the other end of the camp. Again we ran, but as we got closer, I told everyone to stop. "He's going to kill all the cows!" I told my brother. And I think this is where school thinking comes in. I told him, "Look. If we keep on chasing this lion, he's going to kill more and more. So why don't we let him eat what he has now, and tomorrow morning we will go hunting for him."

My brother said, "Yes, that's a good idea," and it was agreed. For the first time I felt like I was part of the brotherhood of warriors. I had just made a decision I was proud of.

It was muddy, it was dark, we were in the middle of nowhere, and right then we had cows that were miles away. They had stampeded in every direction, and we could not protect them. So we came back to camp and made a big fire. I looked for my shoes and I found them. By that time I was bruised all over from the cows banging into me, and my legs were bloody from the scratches I got from the acacia thorns. I hurt all over.

We started talking about how we were going to hunt the lion the next day. I could tell my brother was worried and wanted to get me out of danger. He said, "Listen, you're fast, you can run. Run and tell the people at the other camps to come and help. We only have three real warriors here; the rest of you are younger."

"No way," I said. "Are you kidding me? I'm a warrior. I'm just as brave as you, and I'm not going anywhere." At this point, I hadn't actually seen the lion, and I absolutely refused to leave.

My brother said, "I'm going to ask you one more time, please go. Go get help. Go to the other camp and tell the warriors that we've found the two lions that have been terrorizing everyone, and we need to kill them today."

And I said, "No, I'm not going."

So he said, "Fine," and sent the youngest boy, who was only about eight.

WHEN DAYLIGHT CAME, I took the little boy's spear and walked out from the camp with the others. Barely 200 yards away were the two lions. One had its head right in the cow, eating from the inside. And one was just lying around: She was full. As we approached them, we sang a lion song: "We're going to get the lion, it's going to be a great day for all of us, all the warriors will be happy, we'll save all our cows."

As we got closer, the older man who was with us kept telling us to be careful. We should wait for help, he said. "This is dangerous. You have no idea what lions can do." But no one would listen to him.

The other guys were saying, "We can do it. Be brave, everyone." We were encouraging each other, hyping ourselves up.

My brother was so angry, so upset about our mother's favorite cow that he was crying. "You killed Ngoneya," he was saying. "You are going to pay for it."

Everyone was in a trance. I felt that something inside me was about to burst, that my heart was about to come out. I was ready. Then we came face-to-face with the lions. The female lion walked away, but the male stayed. We formed a little semicircle around the male, with our long spears raised. We didn't move. The lion had stopped eating and was now looking at us. It felt like he was looking right at me. He was big, really big. His tail was thumping the ground.

He gave one loud roar to warn us. Everything shook. The ground where I was standing started to tremble. I could see right into his throat, that's how close we were. His mouth was huge and full of gore from the cow. I could count his teeth. His face and mane were red with blood. Blood was everywhere.

The lion slowly got up so he could show us his full presence. He roared again. The second roar almost broke my eardrums. The lion was now pacing up and down, walking in small circles. He was looking at our feet and then at our eyes. They say a lion can figure out who will be the first person to spear it.

I edged closer to my brother, being careful not to give any sign of lifting or throwing my spear, and I said, "Where's that other camp?"

My brother said to me, "Oh, you're going now?" He gave me a look—a look that seemed to say, You watch out because someone might think you are afraid.

But I said, "Just tell me where to go." He told me. I gave him my spear. "It will help you," I said, and then I took off in the direction of the other cattle camp. No warrior looked back to see where I was going. They were all concentrating on the lion.

As I ran toward the next camp, I saw that the little boy had done his job well. Warriors were coming, lots of them, chanting songs, asking our warriors to wait for them. The lion stood his ground until he saw so many men coming down, warriors in red clothes. It must have seemed to him that the whole hillside was red in color.

The lion then started to look for a way out.

The warriors reasoned that the lion had eaten too much to run fast and that the muddy ground would slow him up. They thought they could run after him and kill him. They were wrong. As soon as they took their positions, the lion surged forward and took off running. The warriors were left behind. There was nothing they could do except pray that they would meet this lion again.

From that time on, I knew the word in the village was that I had run away from the lion. There was no way I could prevent it.

"You know the young Lekuton warrior?"

"Yeah."

"He was afraid of the lion."

My brother tried to support me, but in our society, once word like that gets out, that's it. So I knew that I'd have to prove myself, to prove that I'm not a coward. So from then on, every time I came home for vacation, I went to the cattle camp on my own. I'd get my spear, I'd get my shoes. Even if it was 30 miles from the village, I'd go on my own, through thick and thin, through the forest and deserts. When I got there I'd take the cattle out on my own. Always I hoped something would attack our cattle so I could protect them.

Chapter 2
The Proud One

My age-mates know my bravery.
They say I am a lion.
I roar day and night.

MY PEOPLE SPEAK the Maa language, which is why we
are called Maasai. There are many subgroups within
the Maa culture, including mine, the Ariaal. The Ariaal
is actually a mixture of two groups, the Samburu and
the Rendille. My mother is Rendille; my father was
Samburu. We're nomads: We live where it's best for the
cattle, where there's good grass and water, away from
disease and pests. If the grass runs out or the water dries
up, we move. If there's better grazing land somewhere
else, we move.

A warrior may walk 25 or 30 miles in a day to scout

out new grazing land. He'll just get up and go. He'll go look to see if the grass is good and for signs of predators or people who may want to steal the cattle. Then he'll walk back. Even at night, he'll know exactly where he is. He'll smell the trees and know that a particular tree grows in that place, or he'll hear a certain bird and know exactly where that bird lives. When he returns, he'll discuss what he's seen with the family or the village, and they'll decide whether to move the herd.

The Maa speakers used to live all over Kenya, from north to south. Nairobi—the name of the capital city, in the south—is a Maa word that means "cold." My great-great-grandfather used to graze his cattle as far south as Nakuru, 300 miles from where we live now. Today there are more people, more towns, more boundaries. There are national parks. It's harder to move around, and we live in a smaller area in the north. There are several thousand Ariaals. I don't know the exact number because we don't count people. It's taboo; it's considered greedy. Even when the government census takers come, we don't give them a number. My mom looks the other way and gives them names. She says, "My kids are so, so, and so . . ."—but she doesn't give them a number. She lets them figure it out.

I was born at the end of the rainy season, so everything

was green. People were happy. They didn't have to work too hard. The kids didn't have to take the cattle too far to graze. No one had to go too far to get water; the water was everywhere. This was in the Marsabit district, just south of the border with Ethiopia. It's an area of low rolling hills. The lowlands are dry—almost a desert—but the hills are cooler and wetter, especially during the rainy season. At that time, my village was on the side of a small hill called Kamboe.

Before I was born, my family was made up of my father, my father's two wives—my other mother and my mother—a much older brother named Paraikon, who was my other mother's son and who became a father to me when my father died, and my two older brothers, Ngoliong and Lmatarion, who were eight and five years old. Ngoliong and Lmatarion used to help my mother a lot. Most families have girls, and the girls will go get water or go get firewood. But there were no girls in my family, so my brothers would do that, and people would laugh at them. The girls in the village would laugh and say, "Look at them. They're doing the work of a woman." But my whole family, we just love our mom so much, so my brothers sacrificed their pride and brought water and wood and did other chores. But you can be sure of one thing: Both of them wanted a girl to be born next time. Not my father. He wanted a boy because boys take care of the cattle—he'd have another herder. But my brothers and my mother wanted a girl.

Our hut was under an acacia tree that still stands today. When my mother was pregnant, right up until the time of labor, she would go out and do chores. The evening I was born, she was part of the group of women who went to get firewood. Some of the midwives told her not to, but she likes to work so she went anyway.

That same evening a bull separated itself from the herd and came up to my mother's hut. It was a bull from a cattle family we still have today. He never came to my mother's hut, never. But that day he showed up and rubbed himself on the hut. And one of the elders said: "A baby boy is coming, whether you like it or not."

About midnight—when the night is equal, as the elders say—my mom started to go into labor. Women came with herbs and other things. And when I was born, someone ran outside and said to my father, "Hey, Lekuton! *Ti wa lashe!*" "Baby bull!" In my language, when a child is born, we don't say "boy" or "girl," but *lashe*, which means "male cow," or *ngache*, which means "female cow."

My father made his signature sound: *Hhehh!* Every man has a signature, a sound he makes when he wants to be known. Right now, if I came to my mother's hut in the middle of the night and I wanted my mom to identify me, I would make this sound: *Harumph.* And my mom would say, "That is my son." Even if it's after ten years. So my father made his *Hhehh!* and he said, "Yes, another herder is coming." And my mother and my brothers? They were mad, because they knew that now they'd have to work a little harder to bring a little more wood and water.

My mom thanked the Creator all the same, and all these women came and started singing. When a baby is born in the village, it's a big celebration. But there was a complication. Although it was the rainy season and everything was green, there was disease in the area, and people were worried about the cattle. A few days before I was born, the village had held a meeting and agreed that, with grass and water everywhere, it would be a good time to move. Now, the village can't move the day after a baby is born, so they had to call another meeting of the elders.

"Hey, you know Lekuton's wife has given birth to a baby boy," they said. "It's a blessing, and we must postpone a day or two. And then we have to move." They talked and decided that in two days they'd move.

Another problem was that I refused to breast-feed.

I didn't want anything to do with it. For us, as in America, it's known to be healthy to breast-feed. But I just couldn't do it. So one woman said, "Oh! *Lemasolai!*" "Proud one." That's how I got my name: Lemasolai. He's proud, he refused to breast-feed.

They tried every trick. They tried offering me cows: Our people believe even an infant understands about the cattle. "Take that cow!" my father said. "I'll give you that cow! And I'll give you that other one, too, if you breast-feed!" But I didn't listen.

At the time, there was a little cow that had lost its mom. It slept in the hut with us and some of the little goats. My father had made a leather bottle to feed the calf with, and one woman said, "Hey, why can't he share with the calf?" So I grew up drinking from the same bottle as that little cow. A lot of kids made fun of me, and I put on a lot of weight because I got a lot of cream from the cow instead of getting milk from my mom. But my family gave me that cow. It was the first one I owned.

Two or three days later, the village moved. I was put in a special carrying case made of cowhide and bamboo and placed on top of a donkey. My mother walked beside me. We traveled for a whole day to another area. So really, my life as a nomadic child started when I was three days old.

Chapter 3
Cows

My roar is like thunder.
My cows have nothing to fear.
Fear rests with the cowards,
The cowards of the enemy camp.

MY EARLIEST MEMORY is of sitting outside our hut. I was
probably three and a half or four. It was a sunny day, and
around me the women were busy breaking camp. My
mom was taking down our hut, getting ready to move.
I was playing with rocks. I was just starting to learn the
names of our cows, and I was lining the rocks up and
calling them in, the way my father and brothers did with
the real cows. There was a knife lying on the ground. I
picked it up to play with, and all of a sudden—blood!
It didn't bother me—there was no pain, just lots of
blood. Then someone saw me. "Hey, look at Lekuton's

son!" My mother came running over. She started crying, and then of course I started crying, too. The wound healed—my mother treated it with some herbs—but I still have the scar, under my right eye.

Cows are our way of life. They give us milk and blood and sometimes meat to eat and hides to wear. They're our wealth. We don't have money; we have cows. The more cows somebody has, the wealthier he is. My mother has lived her whole life in a hut made of sticks and cow dung, and you could put everything she owns on the seat of a chair. She lives entirely on the cow. For her, there's something wrong with someone who doesn't have cows. It's just not civilized.

With cows comes respect. The more cows a man has, the more respect he gets. A man with a big herd will be listened to by the others in the village. But if that man loses his cows because he doesn't care for them properly, or is too lazy to take them to better pastures, no one will pay attention. The respect goes with the cows; a poor man does not have a voice. The reason? We know someone with a lot of cows has worked hard, taken risks, brought his cows to where there is grass and water.

We have three criteria for judging a cow. Number one is the color. The best color is white with a lot of black spots, like an Appaloosa horse. To us, that is the most beautiful cow. Number two is the horn. We like a male cow to have big, even horns. And number three is the personality of a cow. A good cow is always at the front of the herd. If the cow is always late, if he's always behind all the other cows, he's not considered a good cow. We do not care about how heavy a cow is. Never. Just the beauty of its color, the size of its horns, and how active it is.

We name our cows. Each cow has a name, like a person, almost. My brother knows the names of all his cows, all of them. At night when he walks home after taking care of his cows, he will stand on raised ground and look down at them.

The cows all belong to different cattle families, and those in the same family look alike. My brother knows how many cows are in each family, and he'll name the families as they pass: Mongo, Muge, Narok, and so on. And he'll know if each family is complete. The Mongo family is all there, the Muge family is all there, the Narok family is all there, and so on. That's how we count. In a few minutes he'll know who is there and who is missing. And that's hundreds of cows.

Our cows do not die of old age. We either sell a cow or butcher it. The only exception is a blessed cow. Right now, one of our cows—it is my brother's cow, a bull—is blessed. It doesn't look like much. It's gray with a single black spot right in the middle of its back. One horn is normal; the other is crooked. But it's special.

Twice it happened that when my brother took his cows out in the morning that bull got in front of the rest of the cows and refused to move. He refused to move until my brother took his cows in a different direction from the rest of the village herd. The first time it happened, my brother didn't understand what the cow was up to, but he is smart, he knows that sometimes cows can have a sense of danger, an instinct. So he went the direction the bull wanted to go. And both of those days raiders—men with guns—attacked the rest of the village herd. But my brother's cows were spared.

That kind of bull is a great blessing. You never can sell one like that. When it gets too old, perhaps 20 or so years old, you can slaughter it in a special ritual in your *boma*, the corral that surrounds the cows at night. Only your family is allowed to eat the meat from that blessed cow. No one else. No one else but a member of your family is allowed to sleep on its hide either.

IT'S CUSTOMARY for the men to take care of the cattle and the women to take care of the village. If you came to the village during the day, you'd find only women and young children. The men and older boys would be out grazing cattle. But when they are very young, boys and girls work and play together.

From about age five to about age seven, I went every day with a group of about a dozen boys and girls to take the young cows to get grass nearby, maybe a mile or so from the village.

Even as little kids, we were smart. We'd drive the young cows to a place where we knew there was a lot of grass. We knew where the wild animals were, so we tried to avoid them. We let the calves graze, fill their bellies. While they ate, we played. But all the time we were watching. Our ears were always open for any danger.

We were proud to be doing our job, but we were little kids. What we really liked to do was play. We boys practiced throwing our little stick spears. We pretended to be warriors. We wrestled in the dust. With the girls we played house. We would arrange rocks in a circle to make a hut. Then we'd pretend we were the parents. The boys would ask the typical questions an elder would ask his wife when he comes home.

"Mama, how's the evening? Did all the cows come home safely?"

"Yes."

"Good. Are all the kids healthy?"

"Yes."

"How about such-and-such cow, the one that is sick? How is he doing?"

"He's doing great. We treated him today, and it looks like he is going to get well."

"Uh-huh. Did you get any visitors today?"

"Yes, your friend came to see you. He was in the neighborhood, only 20 or 30 miles away, so he walked over looking for you. I told him you weren't here, but he said that's fine, he will come back tomorrow. It's only 20 miles. He needs to talk to you about something. Now sit down and have some tea."

Then we would sit in front of a stone and pretend we were eating our supper. The girl would bring me a little stick and we'd pretend it was a cup and go *slurp, slurp, slurp.*

"Okay, I'm going now," I'd say, "I have to attend an elders' meeting. I'll see you later."

Then the boys would sit together and pretend they were elders. We knew what to say because whenever the elders met, we were hiding in the bushes listening.

"We have to move because this location is not good for our cows anymore," one elder would say. "We have to move because three cows have died here."

Then the elders would discuss where to move. One elder would say, "Oh, I want to move to that big rock in the distance. That's where my grandfather is buried. It is a very good area for cows."

Another would say, "No, that area is not very good because of this and this and this." So they'd argue and argue until they reached agreement or disagreement. If the discussion ended in agreement, fine, everyone would move together. If it ended in disagreement, one group would move one place and another would move to another place. The elders always tried hard to reach an agreement, but if they couldn't, they would go in different ways, but they would reunite at a later time. They would always stay friends.

When we played, we were always checking on the little cows to make sure that none of them had wandered off. We all knew we'd be in big trouble if we lost one. Then around noon we brought them into the shade so they could sleep. Calves need to nap, just like people do. Once the cows were asleep, we knew they were safe, so we went back to our play.

THE AFTERNOON always went so fast. Soon someone would say, "Where's the sun? It's getting late. Let's take the cows home." We were still imitating what the elders do. Women in this situation have no say. They just listen. The little girls did the same. They just followed the boys. So we drove our little cows home.

Now we were really dirty, just covered in dust because of all the running around and wrestling we had done. But my parents didn't mind. When I got home, they would say, "Son, congratulations. You brought all your little cows home. Drink some tea and eat something."

Then at about seven o'clock, as the sun was going down, my family put all the calves into the family enclosure, and my job was to stand at the gate to keep them separate from their mothers.

Then my mom would say, "Mongo. Let Mongo get out." I would open the gate, and Mongo, who had heard his name, would come running out to his mother.

The mother cows have four teats. When the little cow ran to its mother to drink milk, my mom would let it suck from two teats, and she would milk the other two teats. In other words, the calf got half, and we got half.

When my mother finished milking that one, she would call, "*Ntei* Mongo!" I'd bring the first calf back to the pen, open the gate, and let the next one out. Letting the little cows get their milk takes about an hour.

My mom used to let me drink my milk right there.

I would sit by the cow and drink my milk out of the teat. The milk is warm and very sweet, much sweeter than milk in America. The sweetness comes from the leaves the cows eat. If we want sweeter milk, we take our cows to special places where they can eat leaves from a certain tree and a certain grass. Then the milk is especially delicious. It carries the scent of the tree.

We also mix cow blood with the milk. This is especially tasty and good for you. Usually it takes three people to get the blood from a cow. Two people tie a rope around the cow's neck and hold it so that the jugular vein pops up. The third person chooses a spot on the vein and hits it with a small, blunt arrow, making a little hole, a horizontal slit in the jugular vein. The blood comes out of that hole. You hold a gourd next to the cow's neck, and the blood pours into the gourd. When you get enough, you loosen the rope and the blood stops flowing. You then put a little medicine on the wound to speed the healing. Having blood taken out isn't bad for the cow. We don't take any more blood than it can spare.

When you have a bowl full of blood, you take a stick and swirl it around in the blood for five to ten minutes to remove all of the clots. Then you mix the blood with milk, more milk than blood. It's delicious, simply delicious. If somebody's sick and needs more blood in his body, we give him more blood than milk in the mixture. We believe that blood goes to blood in the body.

WHEN THE CHORES ARE DONE, the kids get to play some more. We loved that time of day. It was dark, and there were so many night sounds—of birds, animals, insects. They all seemed to be singing to us. It was a great time to tell stories. We'd tell each other stories, and sometimes we would all gather to listen to a grown-up tell stories. My mom is a great storyteller. Often all the kids in the village would come and sit outside our house when it got dark, hoping she would tell a story. I would always sit close to my mom in case the story was scary. Sometimes she would tell a ghost story. The scariest was about the gambit, an animal that had four mouths. When she told gambit stories, all the kids would crowd around her. As the story got really scary, everyone would squeeze in closer. By the end of the story, all of us kids would be in one tight huddle around my mom.

At ten or ten thirty, the kids went to their homes, all excited about the things we'd done and the stories we'd heard, looking forward to the next day's adventures.

Chapter 4
The Pinching Man

My camp is full of fearless warriors,
The warriors of my generation.

SOME PEOPLE MIGHT SAY our society is primitive, but
I think it is the best, fairest system that I know. Our
system is based not only on the family, but also on the
village itself. No one goes hungry. We take care of each
other. We watch out for one another. Children respect
their elders. If children do wrong, any adult can correct
them. That means everyone in the village is equal.

In almost every village there is a disciplinarian
called the "pinching man." He punishes disobedient kids
by pinching them. He pinches you really hard on the
legs, and let me tell you, once you are pinched you
remember it! Parents who want their children to obey

will tell them, "If you don't behave, I will call the pinching man." That usually does the trick. Kids are so scared of the pinching man.

The pinching man in each village is a scary person. Sometimes he has long, pointy fingernails, or hair on his face. He chews tobacco and looks mean. Our pinching man was the worst one of all. You never wanted to be on his bad side, because then he would watch for you, and he would tell the pinching men in the other villages to watch for you, too. And parents rarely protect their kids from the pinching man because that is how discipline is enforced in the community.

A rule I often broke was the one against going to other villages by myself. We nomads live in an area with dangerous animals and poisonous snakes. Our villages are usually miles apart from each other—two, three, four—so kids are not encouraged to go to other villages to play. It is simply too dangerous. But I always liked to play with friends in the different villages.

One day when I was little, about six or seven years old, I was sent out with the calves as usual, but I told one of my friends, "Watch my cows for me a little while, because I want to go play with one of my friends in the next village." I always returned the favor by taking care of other kids' calves if they wanted to go somewhere.

The village I wanted to visit that day was two or three miles away. A narrow, winding path through the woods led there. I took off running, but I had not gotten very far when I turned a corner in the path and came face to face with the pinching man. As soon as he saw me, he crouched down and put out his hands toward me. His fingernails were long and dirty and sharp. Tobacco juice was dripping from the hair on his chin. He was waving his hands, ready to pinch.

When the pinching man gets you like that you cannot run away because he will remember you. The next time he sees you, he will grab you when you are not looking and pinch you even harder.

"Where are you going?"

I had to think fast. "My mother asked me to get some sugar for tea at the next village, also some tea leaves if they have them," I said.

"This time of day?"

I said, "Oh, yes, yes, she wants the sugar right away, and she told me to run."

He looked at me and said, "Well, I was just going to your house, so I will ask her."

"Fine," I said, and I walked past him, but as soon as he couldn't see me anymore, I left the path and cut through the woods as fast as I could to get to my mother's hut before he did. I didn't care if elephants or rhinos killed me. I was more scared of him than of any wild animal.

When I got home, I told my mother the truth, the whole story—"Mom, I made a mistake today. I left my cows with the other kids, and the pinching man caught me. Mom, I wanted to play with my friend so much. I haven't seen him in such a long time. I really had to do something with him. Nothing bad was going to happen."

My mom was shocked. "You left our cows with someone else? What kind of a son are you?"

"Please, Mom. Only protect me today. I will never do it again. This is the only time I'll ask you to protect me from the pinching man. Please, Mom. When he comes, just tell him you sent me to get sugar."

"Go!" she said, and I took off to look after my cows.

Sure enough, a little while later, the pinching man showed up at our hut. "Hey, Nkaririe Lekuton, are you home?" he called.

"Yes."

"Can I have some tea?"

"Yes, I am just cooking some. Come in and rest."

While sipping his tea, he said, "Oh, by the way, I just saw your son on the path leaving the village."

"Oh, yes, I sent him to the next village for sugar."

My mom loves me so much. She supported me. That was it, but if I hadn't told my mom, I would have been in trouble twice—with the pinching man and with her.

But I was an active boy, and my mom didn't always protect me. One time I got a whipping from a warrior right outside our hut, and my mom did nothing to interfere. That day, when my friends and I were watching our little cows, I pretended to be one of the village warriors. A little boy would often pretend to be a warrior, someone he admired and wanted to be like, but this was different. I was imitating this particular warrior to make fun of him. I was saying, "Who's this? Who's the ugly warrior? See how he struts?" The kids loved it. They were laughing and laughing, so I did it the whole day. But that night one of the kids told the warrior what I had done. I had been disrespectful of an elder, and that is very bad in our society.

At that time I loved doing things for older people. I liked running to do someone a favor, to get some sugar or tea, or to carry a message. Run, run, I loved to run. When that warrior came to our hut that night and asked for me, that's what I thought he wanted.

"*Ngoto* Lemasolai, Lemasolai's mother," he called.

"Yeah," she answered.

"Where is Lemasolai today?"

"I'm here," I yelled. I knew his voice and figured he wanted me to go to the next village or hut to get some tobacco for him or something like that.

"Come," he said, "I need to send you." So I came out of the hut quickly, and just as I did, he grabbed me. Before coming to our hut he had gone into the forest and cut a long, thin branch. It was like a whip. As soon as he grabbed me, he took the stick and cut the air with it just like a sword. *Swoosh.*

When I heard that sound, I thought, "Oh my!" I did not know if I was going to die or what.

"So, you have been making fun of me all day?"

"No, no, not me," I said.

"Tell me! What did you say! Tell me everything!"

Then he took that stick and, *Phoom! Phoom! Phoom!* He whacked me on my knees, my thighs, my calves, where it would leave no marks. Then he said, "Go." I took off running, and I went to look for my friends. Who could possibly have told on me? We suspected one of the girls we had played with that day. We decided that if she didn't come back the next day with her little cows, she was the one who had told on me. She did not come back for a week.

My mom heard that warrior whip me, but she never said a thing about it. That is part of the discipline, part of the culture. We don't have many disrespectful kids in our villages. I can vouch for that.

Chapter 5
School

I love my age-mates,
Our warriorhood and brotherhood.
We are to be feared
By men and animals.

THE GOVERNMENT OF KENYA had issued a law that every
nomadic family must send one child to school, whether
they liked it or not. My father did not like it. He didn't
have any use for school—he wanted us home, helping
to raise the cattle. A child at school was one fewer child
to work. My father was also very traditional. He wanted
us to grow up in our own culture, among our own
people. But this was a law. The authorities came and
said, "You must send a boy to school. Choose." No one
sent their girls to school, only boys. My father didn't

know what to say. He didn't want to give Ngoliong away. A mother's oldest child always stays at home; he is an important member of the family. And my father could not send me; I was too young. So he was left with no choice but to send my second brother, Lmatarion.

Because the village moved around, sometimes it was close to the school and sometimes it was far away. At that time, it was close—I'd say about a mile away. The school was run by American missionaries. They taught reading and writing and arithmetic; they also taught Christianity and other Western ways of thinking. Lmatarion, who was about 11 years old, was placed in the first grade.

Right from the beginning, he couldn't stand it. He went to school for one day, and on the second day he ran away with a group of other boys. They all went in different directions. Lmatarion hid in a hyena's hole. He later said, "I'd rather be eaten by hyenas than go to school," but fortunately the hyenas had moved out. He stayed in the hole for three days. Finally, the villagers and police found him and brought him home. The police said to my father, "Well, you're not off the hook, you still have to send one."

I'd been paying attention to what was going on, and I said, "I'm here!"

"How old are you?" they asked.

"Eight." Actually, I was only about six. You had to be eight to go to school, but I was very quick talking, and there was no way for the police to know how old I was because we didn't have birth certificates or any other document that recorded when I was born.

The way the government people reckoned a child's age was to ask him to lift his arm, reach over the top of his head, and touch his opposite ear. A small child can't do that: His arms are too short. So they asked me, "Touch!" and I stretched, put everything into it, and just about reached—or at least got close enough to satisfy the police. It solved a problem for them and for my father and my brothers.

I wanted to go to school. At that time, I was very heavy and the kids picked on me. I was tired of it and eager for any change. So the next day, off I went. When I got there, the American woman who ran the school looked at me and asked, "How old are you?"

I said, "Eight."

She said, "Touch!" and again I reached, really put everything into it. I convinced her, too. Then she gave me a piece of candy. I'd never had candy before. It was so sweet, so good. From then on, she gave me a candy every day. Sometimes I went to her door very early in the morning and waited for the candy. It was like magic. I stayed and never left.

I WAS PUT right into first grade. The school was very simple. There were no chairs, no desks. The teacher had a blackboard, and we sat on the ground. The school day was long, starting at seven in the morning and running until four or five in the afternoon.

We learned the same things in school that children learn all over the world—reading, writing, arithmetic. At first we didn't have paper and pencil, so we learned to write with a stick in the dirt floor of the school.

Another thing we learned was the Bible. I got to know the Old and New Testaments very well, and I learned a lot of Christian values from the missionaries at that school. I still follow those values.

School was so different from life in the village and the cattle camp. The first thing we were told when we arrived was to take off our traditional clothes—our nanga and beads. The missionaries supplied us with uniforms instead: shorts, a shirt, shoes, sometimes a jacket. And I was baptized at the school, which is how I got the name Joseph. But when I went home during the holidays, I changed back into my traditional dress, put on my beads, painted my body. For one thing, the other kids would have teased me if I hadn't. But even at that age, I didn't want to be set too far apart from my culture. I wanted to learn, but I wanted to remain part of the tradition I'd grown up in.

School was tough. The teachers expected a lot from you. They expected you to pay attention and work hard, and to sit still and not cause trouble. It didn't help that I was overweight. The kids at school were just as bad as the village kids. They called me "Kimbo," which is the name of a brand of cooking oil sold in East Africa. It was like being called "Crisco" in the United States. When kids picked on me, I fought back, so I was always in trouble.

A part of every school day was set aside for punishing troublemakers, and I was often one of them. The teacher would call us up in front of the whole school: "Noise-makers, here! Now!" They used corporal punishment— they beat us on the behind with a stick. It was painful, but it didn't stop me. Instead, I found an old pair of shorts and started wearing two pairs, one inside the other. Eventually, I was called up in front of the school again over something I'd done, but this time when the stick came down, I didn't yell, I didn't make a sound. One, two—nothing. I was being brave, showing off in front of the other kids. Three, four—not a sound! But the spare shorts I was wearing were old and dirty, and by this time dust was flying everywhere.

"How many shorts do you have on?" the teacher asked.

"One."

Five, six—the stick came down again.

"How many shorts?"

"Two, sir!"

"Go and take one off!"

So I went to the bathroom and took one pair off, and I was punished pretty severely afterward. But I didn't give up. The next time, I wore two pairs of shorts, and I put a piece of cardboard in between them. But when you hit a piece of cardboard with a stick it makes a loud noise, and sure enough when I was called up to be punished—*Smack!* You could have heard the sound a half mile away! Of course the teacher knew right away what I had done. But instead of being angry, he laughed.

"You're lucky," he said. "This is your lucky day. Go and remove the cardboard, but be good in the future." So that time I got off without a beating.

EVENTUALLY I LEARNED how to deal with the bullies who were always getting me in trouble. There was one in particular: Addison. He was my height, but very strong. He used to bully everybody, even kids who were older and bigger. Because of my weight and my big mass of curly hair that the kids made fun of, and because I was younger than the others, I was an easy target for Addison. He made me carry his bags for him. He took my food at mealtimes. But the last straw for me came at the end of the year. During the last week of school, prizes were given to the top students. Even though I was often in trouble, I liked the schoolwork and was good at it, so at the end-of-year assembly there I was: Joseph Lemasolai Lekuton, receiving a prize for being one of the best in the class. The prize was a pair of good tennis shoes from America.

Addison was waiting for me. On the way out of the assembly, he took the shoes.

"Fine," I said. "Take the prize. Just take it." I was furious. "But leave me alone."

"Don't you tell anyone," said Addison. "If you tell Mama" —Mama was the American headmistress—"if you tell Mama, you'll pay the price. We're going home in a few days. I'll make you carry my bags, and I'll make it harder for you by making you carry a log, too."

I hadn't complained to a teacher about Addison all year, but this time was different. I went to Mama, and she must have believed me, because Addison got punished, and I got the shoes back.

But that wasn't the end of it. He didn't do anything for a couple of days. Then on the last day, when everybody was leaving, Addison took the shoes again. "You know what, Joseph? I'm ready for a fight. One o'clock, down by the river." And he announced it to the whole school, so there was really no way out for me.

When I got there, kids were gathered in a circle: big kids—Addison's friends—on one side, and little kids— the kids Addison bullied—on the other. Addison was sure he was going to beat me up.

"Look at this stupid boy," he was saying. "Look how fat he is. Look at that big Afro. You think he can fight me?"

I was so mad, I didn't wait. I just dove at his legs. He wasn't ready. He was standing off guard, bragging, daring me to come toward him, and—*bang!* He hit the ground, headfirst. As soon as he landed, I jumped on top of him and started pounding him. I guess my weight helped. And that was it: fight over. As soon as I let him go, Addison took off. He had learned to swallow some of his own medicine, and I was working toward being a warrior.

ONE OF THE PROBLEMS the nomads have with school is that we move our villages and the cattle, but the school stays in one place. That means leaving the children behind. The first year, my village was near the school, and I was able to go home easily. In my second year, the missionaries built a dormitory and started a boarding school. My family could move wherever they wanted to, and I could stay in school.

My mom used to visit sometimes. She'd bring me milk. The food at school wasn't what I was used to, and there wasn't much of it. We ate mostly corn and beans—yellow corn, from America. Once I counted mine: There were 75 pieces of corn and 15 beans—so little it barely covered the plate. I didn't complain—I was grateful for the school and the missionaries—but I was a nomadic kid, raised on milk. So whenever my family was nearby, my mother would bring me some milk. Sometimes she'd walk 10 or 20 miles with it.

I went to that school through the seventh grade. Every time school closed for the vacation, I had to find my way home. That was one of the hardest things: The village might be 5 miles away, or it might be 50. Sometimes I wouldn't know exactly where my family was. I had to search for them. So I'd set out with some other boys from my area. Sometimes the school car would take us to a point on the road as close as it could to where we were going. Then we'd walk. Usually, there would be plenty of people along the way, in villages and cattle camps. We could spend the night with any family. If we didn't encounter any people, we'd find a cave or sleep in a tree. The longest it took me to find my own family was about two weeks.

I'll tell you a story about a journey home when I was about ten. At that time, our village was really far away from the school, near the northern border of Kenya. About 80 of us boarded a truck. Most of the students were from other clans, very few from my village. The truck took us to a place called Nolongoi. It's not even a place, really. It's just a big acacia tree by the road. The truck stopped, and we all got out. And home was still 40 miles ahead.

With us were some older boys. They were almost in their 20s but were going to school late because their fathers were forced to send someone. Those boys were our leaders. And their families were even farther away than mine. First we would walk to my village, and then they would continue on to theirs—another 25 miles or so. And it was raining, so we were all pretty miserable.

My suitcase was a plastic garbage bag. I had been given a real suitcase by the missionary women in school, but it had broken apart in the rain one day. So now I carried a plastic bag with the few clothes I had in it.

So we started walking. The terrain was flat with acacia trees, small bushes, and a few rocks that increased as we went farther into the lowlands. The ground was muddy from all the rain, and the mist made it hard to see where we were going. We were hungry—so hungry. And then I was afraid, because all around us as we walked along were fresh elephant and buffalo tracks.

All of a sudden, the older boys who were leading called, "*Shh!* Stop! Everybody, get down!" So we all crouched down. There in front of us was a large herd of elephants—dozens. Something had alarmed them. They were scared and running in our direction. One of the older guys, Mogole, picked me up and put me on his back. He was two classes ahead of me, and big—probably six feet tall. When my mom brought milk to the school for me, she always brought some for him as well. He had become a good friend of mine. Someone in our group whistled. Elephants hate a whistle, and they shifted direction when they heard it. Then we got out of there.

We all ran and hid in a cave because there was more to worry about than the elephants. From the cave we could see back the way we'd come—could watch to see what had startled those elephants. Sure enough, we soon spotted two men with guns and tattered clothes. *Shiftas.* They were coming in our direction.

There are a lot of shiftas in Kenya—poachers who kill wild animals for money. As soon as we saw them, we knew we had to get away. Poaching is a serious crime, and shiftas are dangerous if they think someone has seen them at work. Luckily, the older guys figured out a way to go around the hill. It was probably five miles out of our way, but we managed to escape. Even then everyone was uneasy. Some boys kept insisting they could see people ahead of us, but it always turned out to be tree stumps they were seeing.

We finally reached home at six or seven in the evening. It was about 40 miles, but we had covered it in about 12 hours because we were running most of the time. I took the older boys to my mother's hut, because we have a lot of cattle and a lot of milk. They drank and rested, and the next morning they left for their own village.

The next day we heard that the shiftas had found our tracks and followed us right to the edge of the village. That's just one of the many dangers I encountered when I went to school.

A LOT OF KIDS didn't stay in school. Some ran away; some just didn't return from vacation. People in the village knew they could slowly take their kids out, and no one would follow up. The government had other things to do. Officials wouldn't be asking every year if their kids were in school. But I was allowed to stay on.

When I came home, my brothers would make fun of me. They'd say, "What do you think you're getting in that school?"

When I first started school, my father was always saying to my mother, "Why do you want him to go to school? We want him here. We should take him out."

But my mom would say, "No, no, we can't. No way. We can't have him stay here." She could see I wanted to go. And every time I came home I'd tell stories. I'd bring candy for my brothers, too.

I think the toughest part—tougher than the school, than the food, than walking home—was that gradually I was coming home to people who were not the same as I was anymore. When I got home I could see myself a little bit differently. I'd be taking care of the cattle or talking to my family about different things, and I'd be able to explain how my name was written—I'd show my brothers, and they would try to copy it. Or I could teach them some English, or some math. It's so hard to explain the way it felt to be a little kid with a culture that was mine and another culture that I was learning. But I remember that from the beginning I wanted my culture to be number one and school to be number two—I would learn them both at the same time if I could. The missionaries really did tell me, "Remove those clothes! The beads you're wearing! It's not right!" And at school, that's what I did. But when I got home, I wore my traditional clothes and lived the way my family lives. And I still do.

Chapter 6
Herdsman

Let's praise the brave
And castigate the cowards.

WHEN I WAS ABOUT NINE YEARS OLD, there was a bad
drought in our region. It hadn't rained in almost two
years. Water holes had dried up, and the grass had died.
With so little water available, the nomads had scattered.
My brother Ngoliong had taken our cattle a long way
from the village, to an area called the Kaisut desert. He
was alone there, and since I was home from school on
vacation, I was sent to help him. I got there, and the
sun was scorching—the soil was too hot to walk on.
Everything was dry. The only green things were the
acacia trees, which have long roots that grow deep into
the ground.

Because of the dry conditions, there was very little milk. The cattle just weren't producing very much. So most of the time, we went hungry. When there was milk, we bled a cow, mixed the blood with the milk, and drank it. But when there was no milk, we went hungry.

Within a few days, I realized that things were going to be very tough for me. I was hungry, and I was thirsty. I complained to my brother, but there was nothing he could do. We were both dehydrated, but water was a day's walk away. I felt I might die. I was weak, and I could barely talk. Finally my brother realized that I was in serious trouble.

He told me, "Look at the cattle. Look at the noses of the cows. Do you see liquid there?" He told me that it was water, and that I should lick it. So I carefully chose the good cows, the ones that we thought were friendly, and I licked the sweat off their noses. Right away I began to feel better. I licked the cows' noses every day. I don't know if it was the water, or if it was that my brother had made me believe we could survive out there, but I was okay after that.

SOON I WAS OLD ENOUGH to take the cows out by myself. I was told, "Take the cows to this place, be brave, don't be a child." And I didn't ask any questions. I just got up and went. I left at six or seven in the morning and returned at eight or nine in the evening, depending on the distance to water and grass. I didn't take water or food. If we had food, I ate before I left, drank some tea, and that was it until I came home in the evening. I had my nanga and my spear, nothing else. That's just how it is. It gets hot sometimes, and you don't have any water. It rains, and you stand in the rain. It's cold, and you sit through it. Sometimes you have no shoes, so your feet become strong. They develop shoes of their own.

When I was with the cows, they were my responsibility. I had to protect them. If I didn't, I'd get punished. If an animal killed one of the cows, I'd be in trouble. So I'd find a hill or tall tree and climb it. The cows could graze at the bottom, and I could keep a lookout for thieves or wild animals.

Most of the problems I had were with animals—elephants, buffalo, hyenas. The elephant is dangerous: If it charges, it can kill you. Elephants are fast, really fast. They don't look it, but when you see one running, you can see that their steps are really fast. Long steps, too. And they're so big—a human being is nothing compared with one. But often the elephant just shows off. It charges, it stops, it flaps its ears—tries to scare you.

The hyena is greedy. Once, when Lmatarion was

about 14, he fell asleep under a tree. He woke to the sound of one of the smaller cows in the herd being attacked by a hyena. So he took his spear and went after the hyena—followed it, chased it down, and when he got close enough, speared it right in the stomach. Now the hyena had a bad wound, but it kept running, and as it ran, some of its insides fell out. When the hyena turned around, it saw its guts on the ground and thought: Food. It didn't know that it was its own flesh. It just started eating. That's how greedy the hyena is.

I HAD PLENTY OF FRIENDS in the village, and like me, they spent their days grazing the cattle. Normally my family would tell me, "Take these cows to graze tomorrow in this place," and I'd say, "Okay, Dad, okay, Mom, I'll do that." But sometimes the night before I would talk to my friends, and we'd agree to meet somewhere and play. We'd take our cows out, but at midday we'd gather at the meeting point we'd arranged. We'd all break the rules, but no one knew. We did that many times, but there's an expression in my culture that says, "The day of the thief is the 40th; the 41st day, you get caught." And of course the 41st day did come.

That day we played for too long—climbing trees and seeing who could throw his stick or his spear the farthest. While we were playing, my cows wandered. I didn't notice until we were finished. Then I looked, and I didn't see them. All the other boys' cows were there. I was the only one who was missing his cows. I started tracking them, and pretty soon I found the herd. But five of the cows were still missing. Now I knew I was in big trouble. First of all, I'd lost the cows. Second, when my family asked me, "Where did you lose the cows?" I'd have to give them the true location, and they'd know I did not take them where I was supposed to take them. And now it was getting late.

So I brought all my remaining cows to my friends and asked them to take them home for me. I decided I wasn't going home that night. I knew I'd be punished, and it was embarrassing. I went looking for the lost cows but couldn't find them, so when it got dark I found a very big tree, climbed up, and slept there. All night I could hear people walking by looking for the cows— and looking for me. My mom was totally scared, and eventually the whole village was running around asking, "Have you seen him? Have you seen him?" No one knew what was going on. At about three o'clock in the morning the cows came home by themselves, but I didn't know that. I thought they were lost for good, so when it got light, I was still scared. I spent two nights hiding.

Early on the third day I went to a cattle camp that was not far from our village. One of the older people there had heard that I was missing and sent word to the village. Now I had to face my biggest brother. My father had died when I was about eight years old, and Paraikon, my much older brother from my other mother, was now the head of the family. We all called him Father because that was his place in the family now. I knew he loved me, and he was kind, but he was just as strict as my own father had been.

I decided I'd better not wait for him to find me; I'd go and find him. I'd been hiding long enough, I guess. And I decided I'd be ready to speak for myself. I waited for him where I knew he'd bring the cattle. Eventually, I saw him coming. He was carrying a whip made from a thin tree branch and chewing his knuckles, spitting. I could see his long ears, could see him looking at all the cows.

I went up to him and said, "Father, I have something to show you." I was carrying a sheet of paper. He didn't care. He was looking the other way. But I brought the paper to him and said, "I'm asking for forgiveness, and this is what I learned in school." He took the piece of paper and looked.

"So what does this say?"

"It says, 'I'm sorry for losing the cattle.'"

He looked at me and said, "You know, Son, I've been proud of you for what you've done in school, even though I don't agree with it. And that mistake—you've paid for it by hiding in the woods for two days. You're lucky you didn't get eaten by a lion. So take the cows out today, and take them to that place I told you."

I could see my friends hiding behind a small rock, looking to see what was going to happen to me. They knew that morning was the time the grown-ups usually get you. If they punish you in the morning, they know you'll be taking care of those cows very well for the day. And I said, "Yes, sir, I know where it is. I'll take them there today and make sure that they graze well and that nothing happens to them."

"We'll talk in the evening when you come home."

At that point I didn't want to see my friends at all, didn't want to have anything to do with them. I just wanted to be on my own. I took the cows, and I grazed them. And when I brought them home their bellies were full.

Father told me, "Come." He took me to the cows, looked them over, and said, "This is Sile. She has got three calves—that one, that one, that one. They're yours." And I tell you, I could not believe it. A gift of cows shows great respect.

It showed that my biggest brother loved me. And it was smart. Because from then on, every time I took the cows out to graze I made sure to take them where there was a lot of grass, because some of them were mine.

▲ Here I am a Maasai warrior, holding my club and wearing my traditional clothes and some of my finest beads. Although I have accomplished much in the Western world, I will never forsake my cultural heritage. My goal is to help the nomadic peoples of Kenya preserve their languages, their cultures, and their traditions and to increase their educational opportunities.

▲ Here I am at an elephant conservatory near Mombasa with the other members of my soccer team. I was attending the school at Voi, preparing to retake the primary exam for admission to high school. This is one of the only photographs I have of myself as a youngster. I am standing in the back row, second from the right. You can see my afro.

◄ This is my mom, the most important person in my life.

▲ Maa warriors always walk in single file. Here I am leading my brothers and cousins near Marsabit.

▲ The women in our village build the houses, which are made of sticks plastered with cow dung.

▲ These women are carrying water all the way from that lake, up the hill, and several miles to their village.

KENYA

SUDAN

ETHIOPIA

0   200 miles

0   200 kilometers

Lake Turkana (Lake Rudolf)

Northern Kenya

Marsabit

MARSABIT NATIONAL RESERVE

UGANDA

K E N Y A

SOMALIA

Kaisut Desert

Isiolo

Equator

•Nakuru

MASAI MARA GAME RESERVE

Lake Victoria

⊛ Nairobi

AFRICA

TANZANIA

•Voi

• Mombasa

Indian Ocean

KENYA

☐ Author's home area

☐ Game Reserve, National Park, or National Reserve

Savanna area

▲ Here is my country, Kenya. I come from the Marsabit district in the north. Because we are always looking for better sources of food and water for our cattle, we move our village often.

▶ Here I am visiting a village near the Masai Mara.

Chapter 7
Initiation

Our clan has no cowards.
They know no limits.
Our cows ceased to be scared when I was a baby.

THE MOST IMPORTANT EVENT of my whole life was my circumcision. In many parts of the world and in many traditions, boys have the foreskin cut back or removed from the glans of the penis. Some cultures feel that a circumcised penis is healthier, some that it is holier. In Maa culture, the circumcision ceremony is the initiation that makes a boy a man.

In the Maa world, a man who is not circumcised is considered a small boy. He cannot make decisions, and anyone can tell him what to do. It doesn't matter how smart he is or how old he is or what he does. He can be a professor. He can be a hunter. He can be a journalist, a cook, he can be anything, but people will not take him seriously if he's not circumcised.

I was circumcised when I was about 13. Ngoliong and Lmatarion, who are 5 and 8 years older than I am, were circumcised at the same time. That's because the circumcisions don't take place every year. They're generally held several years apart—whole generations are circumcised together.

When you're circumcised with a group of people, you always identify yourself as part of that group. So if people ask me what age group I belong to, I say I'm Ilkiroro. If I see somebody of my circumcision group, I think, "I know that guy." He's not necessarily my age—there could be 10 years or more between us—but it's still a sign we're the same generation. There were maybe 200 in my group, from my village and several surrounding villages, ages 12 to 22.

THE FIRST STEP for any group of young men is to ask for circumcision from the elders in the community. The way you ask is to sing songs. The village gathers, and the young men sing songs they've made up themselves—songs praising the elders or their families or the cattle. "Blessed Be the Mother of This Beautiful

Daughter." "May God Give You Long and Beautiful
Life." Then you say: "We need a time for circumcision."

This can be a thing that takes several months and
many songs. Many elders just cry to hear your songs.
They remember what it felt like when they were young,
and they remember their own initiations. They let you
sing and sing and sing. They want you to understand
that manhood doesn't come easily. But eventually they
say yes. They need warriors to defend the village.

The next two steps are called *ilbaa* and *naingure*.
Everyone who is going to be initiated has to go cut
arrows. These arrows are supposed to be straight and
from a specific tree called a *siteti*. Then we have to collect
gum from another tree, called a *silalei*. This gum tree
grows on a hill in the lowlands. At the right time of the
year, when the tree produces its gum, the young men
go there to spend the night and collect it. The gum is
like chewing gum. It smells great, and a lot of people
burn it like incense to make their houses smell good.
But if you put it on the tip of an arrow and leave it, it
gets hard. It becomes like a rock.

After the circumcision, when their wounds are
still fresh, warriors are required to practice their life
skills using these arrows. But the arrow is not supposed
to really pierce the animal: It is just supposed to knock

the prey down. We don't believe in shedding blood at that time.

Also, there's a particular kind of rope used to bind the arrows. It's white and very soft, made from the bark of a specific tree. A warrior's mother collects this material, makes the rope, and ties the arrows in a bundle.

Finally, your mother has to kill two or three goats to make a leather coat for you, because for a month before you're circumcised, you have to wear leather. These goats have to be pure white or pure black—no markings. It's very difficult to get goats like that, so people look for months to find them. All these preparations are not easy, but they are very important. Someone who is not ready will have to wait for the next group to be initiated, which could take 10 or 15 more years.

Now, as the time of my circumcision approached, I was away at school. So I had to do a lot of the preparation there. I spent three or four months making up and learning songs for the elders, then I sang them when I was home for vacation. My brothers and my mother were able to make some of the other preparations for me—collecting sticks and gum for the arrows, collecting the rope to bind them with. That's allowed. All the time I was preparing for my final exams that year, I was preoccupied with what was to come, with being ready.

FINALLY THE DAY CAME. As I said, there were about 200 boys and young men in my group, all ready to be circumcised in one day. A special village—called an *alorora*—was created for the ceremony. Only the families of the boys being initiated were allowed to set up their huts in that village. The rest of the villagers were far away. Early in the morning, about six o'clock, the circumcision started. The best-known, most prominent family always goes first, then the second best-known and so on, down to the least known. My family, the Lekuton family, always goes first because it is huge and because many of my forefathers were leaders. Within the family it goes by seniority, so they started with my father's older brothers' children. My father was one of the youngest of the big Lekuton family, and I was the youngest of the boys in my father's family, so they had to work all the way through my cousins and brothers before it was my turn. I had heard about this ceremony all my life, and then I watched my cousins and brothers, so I knew exactly what to expect. And then it was my turn.

The hard thing is, while the ceremony is going on you're not allowed to move your body an inch. You can't twitch your finger or move your mouth. Even your eyelashes have to stay absolutely still. There were three people there to support me. I sat on a skin on the ground with my legs spread out, and one man held my back up strong. The other two men gently held my legs steady.

Not everything was gentle, though. My other mother was there with a club. My other mother loved me to pieces, but she stood ready to clobber me if I moved. That was her job, to make sure I wasn't a coward. My mom was there, too, but she's not as tough as my other mother. And the rest of my family was all around me, to show solidarity and to make sure I didn't embarrass them.

Then came the man with the knife. He danced in front of me, spitting and waving his knife in the air to scare me. This is one of the rituals. My family poured water mixed with milk—considered a blessing—in my face, and some bubbles settled right on my eyelashes. If those bubbles dropped, it would show that I'd twitched my eye. No blinking! For seven, eight, or ten minutes, or however long it takes, no blinking, no movement, my eyes open but as still as a rock. He took the knife, made the first cut, and it felt like my head was split down the middle. The pain was nowhere else, it was right in the middle of my head.

It's believed that if you survive the first three cuts, it will change your life. And there were my brothers, already circumcised, saying, "Don't blink. Don't move.

Don't bring embarrassment to our family. We've never been embarrassed before." Meanwhile, the operation continued. Eight, nine minutes. It's a complicated process, so how long it takes depends on how good the circumciser is. If he's not so good, too bad for you, you have to go for ten minutes or more. If he makes a mistake, you have to wait for him to fix it—you have no choice, you cannot leave. As the initiation was going on, I could hear songs coming from every part of the village. Songs of bravery and brotherhood, songs of the clan.

Finally, after probably seven or eight cuts, I heard my mother let out a loud breath—a sigh of relief. I could hear the other boys singing for me: "He's done it. He is part of us now. He went through it." My other mother put down her club.

Then the circumciser hit me on the thigh with the flat side of the knife. He said, "Wake up. You're a man now. You're a man." You have to hear that. From that time on, your world has changed forever. At that time, it felt like heaven had opened and everything was clear, except the pain was getting worse by the minute.

I didn't get up until I was given all the cows I'd earned. As soon as you pass the test, you're allowed to ask for cows from everyone in your family who is present. I got 22 that day. Then they carried me to my mother's hut, where there were two big beds made of branches and covered with skin. I lay down on top of that skin, and the pain just kept coming on. There is no medicine, no painkiller. You just go through it. I could hear my brothers and other people all around us—"*Ohhhh! Ohhh!*" I was doing that, too. But the worst was over; the healing had started.

WE ALL REMAINED in the village for a couple of months to heal, to grow close to one another, and to get ready for the big feast to celebrate our initiation. Beginning two days after the circumcision, each warrior is supposed to kill birds to make a skin headband. A good headband takes about 15 birds. This is where those special arrows tipped with gum come in. You have to hit the birds with blunt arrows and knock them down. You do this while you're still in pain, still sore. But the good thing is, you don't wear any clothes during this time, especially when hunting. After you kill your birds, you skin them—you have to be good at skinning as well as at shooting—and you line them up on a string.

The problem for me was that I was still young and not very good with a bow. But I had a friend, Nkadaru, who was crippled. He walked with crutches that the missionaries had given him. He was older, in his 20s.

He may not have been able to walk well, but he was a good shot, and he was smart—he knew where to find the birds. We decided to work together.

At this point, the only thing we were allowed to eat was *saroi*. It's milk and blood that's been fermented for days. It's believed to rebuild your blood, and we certainly needed rebuilding because you lose a lot of blood during circumcision. So we brought a gourd of saroi and we camped in a big, big tree. Sure enough, all these birds came out. Nkadaru shot them down, and my job was to run and bring them back. I had to be quick because some would regain consciousness and run away. As soon as they hit the ground, I ran and grabbed them. Then we skinned them—Nkadaru was a very good skinner. We got a lot of birds that way. I had more than 15 on my string. That surprised my brother Lmatarion, who was hunting by himself somewhere else. He got only 12.

THE BIG OCCASION when we were finally recognized as men was a ceremony called *Imuget*. Each new warrior was required to slaughter a cow, and all of the tribe came from many surrounding villages to join the feast. This ceremony marked the end of the long celebrations. During the months that we had spent together, my age-mates and I had formed lifelong friendships.

Cows have special parts. The most important part is the *nkiyeu*, or chest area, because it holds the heart. For the lmuget ceremony, each new warrior selects another warrior who he feels will be a trusted friend forever, one he can confide in during times of hardship and times of happiness. He calls this warrior Nkiyeu and gives him that part of his cow. Then the friends drink together, and that saroi binds them forever. I have two Nkiyeus— Leneepe and Lesamama.

Sitting at that feast with my family and friends, I felt so good. Conquering the circumciser's knife made me feel that I could conquer all the challenges that would ever come my way. I had earned my place in the brotherhood of warriors and could take part in community decisions. I was a man.

Chapter 8
Kabarak

When I was born, a lion was born.
I can kill a lion on flat land and on high land.

BY THE TIME I WAS CIRCUMCISED, I had left the missionary school and was attending a school near Mombasa.
The reason was this: The missionary school was pretty
good—it got me started, gave me a good background—
but when the time came to take the national high
school examination, I didn't get good grades. Most of
the kids there didn't do well. They did okay, but not as
well as kids elsewhere in the country. After all, we were
nomads, far from the capital, Nairobi. We didn't always
get the best teachers, and some of those who came
resented being sent to work in what they thought of as
a remote and backward place. It takes many days for the

teachers to get to our area, and the roads are in poor condition.

I didn't want to be a failure. I'd already left my home and my village and stayed at school. I wanted to keep going, and I wanted to do well. I had started to develop a new ambition toward the end of my time at the missionary school. I'd learned something about government, heard people in power on the radio, but I had never heard anything about our people being in power. Nomads are a minority in Kenya. We continue to live traditionally and haven't been well represented in government or other institutions. I was starting to learn something about that and to think that maybe I could help someday.

As it happened, I had a cousin who worked for Kenya Wildlife at a place called Voi, in southern Kenya near Mombasa. He allowed me to go down and stay with him for a year so I could attend a different school and retake the primary exam. When I did, I got all A's, and I was accepted at a high school called Kabarak. Kabarak was a very prestigious school. It was sponsored by Daniel arap Moi, who was then president of Kenya.

KABARAK IS IN NAKURU, in the Great Rift Valley about 90 miles or so from Nairobi. I was a poor nomadic kid, still very traditional in my outlook and my way of life. I didn't actually wear my red nanga when I went down there for the first time, but I carried it with me. I felt like everyone could see it, like I had the wrong clothes on.

When I got to Nakuru, I found the school and walked up to the gate, but I couldn't bring myself to go in. I just sat down outside, watching the cars drive in. Some of them were pretty fancy cars, too—Mercedes and the like—and there I was, in my old, patched school uniform. I finally got up my nerve. I walked up to the guard and told him I'd come to be a student there. He chased me away. I went back across the street and watched some more. Finally, I went back and showed the guard my admission letter, and he let me in.

Once I got through that gate it seemed to take forever to get to the building where the guard said the new students should report. I was very shabby, with my plastic garbage bag over my shoulder, and everyone was staring. I was so embarrassed it seemed like my legs couldn't carry me. One thing I remember is that I never looked back at the gate. Never. I was so afraid the guard would call me back, tell me I had to leave. I just kept walking until I reached the building.

Some of the other kids were like me, but not really like me. None of them were as ragged, and none of them looked as tired as I felt. I kept thinking about how I had so little money in my pocket, just enough to buy some bread at the canteen.

Someone called out our names, and we were given our uniforms and sent to the dormitory. It was a big room with lots of bunks. I got a lower bunk. It was temporary housing because they were building a new dormitory. It wasn't really very good, but I liked it a lot. No rain came through the roof; it had the best bed I had ever slept on; and there was a shower in a building near the dormitory. I was in heaven.

There were a lot of very wealthy kids at Kabarak. There were some poorer kids too, but even they had some Western, urban ways about them. They'd lived in the city; they spoke incredible English; they had television at home. And there I was—I didn't even know what a television was. I'd never seen one in my life! What I knew about was cows, so we didn't have a lot in common. When I talked about cattle, it was like "What are you talking about?" They just laughed at me. It was culture shock in my own country.

Even though I was different from the other kids, after the first shock, we got along well. I made a lot of friends there, and many of them are my friends today. I realized early on that I was one of the few nomads in the school, and that gave me courage, self-confidence. At vacation time, the other kids at Kabarak went home to the city and hung out. I went to the cattle camp. It gave me an edge. I looked at my experience at Kabarak as another initiation, as part of my preparation for life. Everything you do in our culture, you are preparing for the next stage. Everything you do in life is preparing you for the next challenge.

The kids at Kabarak came from all over Kenya. Many different tribes were represented. It was like a little United Nations. We spoke either English or Swahili to each other. I guess that is how I started relating to people, mixing with all those groups. The elite in numbers and education were the Kikuyu. There were also Luo, Luhya, Kalenjin, Kamba, Digo, and Kisii. And there were a few nomadic students at Kabarak. We were all from different parts of the country. But we were all in the same situation, and we became friends. Some nomadic kids were really embarrassed to say where they were from, but I was proud.

Still, sometimes I would wake up at night and wonder why I was there, why I was doing this. Every day there were little things, little symbols that showed I was not from the right class, that maybe I didn't belong there socially, that maybe I had stepped out of line by leaving my cows and coming to such an elite place. But I tried not to dwell on it. The school treated me like everyone else, and that was the most important thing.

Although no one became a special mentor to me, I became friends with some of my subject teachers. The teachers were very good. Many came from Nairobi, some from Uganda. Two were British, and one was American. The subjects were the same as at a good high school in the United States, although the curriculum was different.

Slowly, I learned what to do and what not to do. One thing was sure: I was going to study really hard. My goal was to be successful and not let my family down. They had had to sell three or four cows to pay the fees when I went to Kabarak. That was a lot of cattle for them—it's an expensive school. And there was a drought at the time, so there were few to spare. A lot of our cows had died that year. The funny thing about it was I don't think they would have felt let down if I had quit and come home. They supported me, but school was not important to them. They would just have thought, well, he's come back to be a herder. Now we'll have enough people to work for us.

But I was determined. The school was intense. Everyone was sharp—if you relaxed, you'd find yourself at the bottom of the class. The curriculum was quite specialized: You had to choose three core subjects and focus on them. Mine were economics, Kiswahili, and geography. That was what I felt comfortable with.

The days were hectic. Wake-up was at 5:30 in the morning. Classes began at 8:00 and went on until about 4:00; then we'd go out for sports. Dinner was at 6:00, and then we'd go back to study until about 9:00. And keeping up with the schoolwork often meant even longer hours—getting up as early as 4:00 in the morning and not going to bed until 10:00 or 10:30 at night, sometimes even later.

Everyone was required to live at school. The kids who came from the wealthier families around Nairobi always complained, but I loved it. I had never lived better. In the third year, I was made a prefect—a student who's given some responsibility for monitoring the other kids and running some school activities—and I had my own room.

I ALWAYS LOVED my holidays at home. But in the days before school closed, I'd have nightmares about how to get there. There was no problem getting from Nakuru to Isiolo. You could take a regular passenger bus. But from Isiolo to Marsabit, the only means of transport was on top of trucks carrying food and other goods to Marsabit. You had to climb up there and hang on. It's about 200 miles, and usually it took a day or two depending upon the condition of the truck you were riding on. Many of the trucks were old and in poor shape. I always tried to find a new one, but sometimes there was no choice. The roads were bad, too—so bad that the trucks were always getting flat tires. And there were bandits. It's a remote stretch of road, and there was always the danger of being attacked and robbed.

Even getting on top of those trucks was a nightmare. The moment I arrived in Isiolo I would start looking for a ride. It was normal to spend four or five days trying. It was even worse during the rainy season, when I could spend a week or two. The road to Marsabit was unpaved, and heavy rains could make it impassable. I never had very much money, and after a day or two looking for transport, I always ran out. Since I didn't know anyone in town, I'd spend the nights sleeping in the open, on the verandahs of shops. It was dirty, and at night it would get very cold. Isiolo has a lot of bars, and people leaving the bars would step on me. Most of the people sleeping on the streets there are homeless kids and orphans. I always felt like one of them when I slept out. I wouldn't get any apology when someone stepped on me, just insults. And then, after a mostly sleepless night, I'd have to get up and start looking for a new ride.

There's a police checkpoint in town. Students looking for rides gathered there, and the police would do their best to help. So long as there weren't too many of us, they would ask the drivers to give us rides. If there were too many, they'd chase us away, so I always made a point to get there early, around 4 a.m. With luck, I'd find a truck and get on my way. But even with luck, I was usually on the road for a week or more before I got home. Most of the other students at Kabarak lived in the big cities; they'd be home within four or five hours of school closing.

Sometimes I'd get desperate. I would think about my mother, my brothers, and my friends, and about the cattle. At home, I could bear hunger and being out in the heat and the rain because I'd be taking care of our livestock. Their beautiful horns and colors could make my hunger disappear. In Isiolo or on top of a truck driving the endless miles up to Marsabit, I sometimes felt like a beggar. But then I'd remember a good grade or something positive I'd achieved, like doing well in soccer, or I'd think about the future, about what I could accomplish for my people with an education, and

I'd find encouragement in that. The elders in the village taught us that a man who has gone through hardships will be the most likely to enjoy success. And it would be a shame and an embarrassment, after so many years of learning, even to think of quitting.

Chapter 9
Soccer

Our cattle have a warrior,
We graze on lions' land.
The lion could have been lucky.

SOCCER CHANGED EVERYTHING for me.

By the time I arrived at Kabarak, I already knew that I would have to compete. I had been competing from the moment I had entered the mission school. In Kenya the students across the country are competing against each other all the time because advancement is limited to the smartest, hardest-working students. You compete to get into high school, and you compete to get into college. A lot of students are left out along the way. In Kenya you are accustomed to competing your whole life.

Academically, things were pretty equal at Kabarak. I worked hard and got good grades, but a lot of students there were getting good grades. The thing that helped me was soccer. I got to meet a lot of students, and I made a lot of friends. Since I was a good soccer player and a responsible student, in my third year the headmaster asked me to be one of the co-captains of the team.

But one game in particular made a difference to me. As I've said, this school was sponsored by the President of Kenya, Daniel arap Moi. He had a house not far from the school, and sometimes he'd come over to see us. One afternoon he walked by during soccer practice. We stopped and ran over to greet him, and he asked me, "Who is soccer captain?"

I said, "I'm one of them, Sir," and introduced myself.

"Well," he said, "next week you have a game against the minister of education's school. You must win that game. It's very important to me." The minister of education also sponsored a school in his area, and every year there was a day of competition between the two.

"Yes, Your Excellency," I said. "We will try."

And he said, "You will not try. You will win!"

I was very competitive, so I answered, "Yes, Your Excellency. We will win."

"Good! Now—do you have any problems?"

"Your Excellency, our uniforms are starting to fade and we have worn-out shoes."

"Okay—I will do something."

The next week, we had new uniforms and shoes.

When Saturday came, there was a lot of excitement. A crowd of people had come to see the games: first basketball, then field hockey, then volleyball, and last of all, soccer. Our school won in field hockey and volleyball, then the other school won basketball. But it was the soccer match, at four in the afternoon, that was the highlight. Students came, parents came, politicians and other dignitaries came. The president was sitting there with the minister of education. The president told us, "Good luck! I hope you win!" And we started the game.

By halftime, we were losing, two goals to nothing. The president came down and spoke to us. "Tell me," he said, "You're the soccer captain?"

"I'm one of them." I told him my name again, a second time, because I knew he was a busy man.

"I want you to win this game. And I'll do something for you. So, go!"

I told him again, "Yes, Excellency! We will win the game."

I had always been a team player, but this time I felt

so much personal pressure from the president. I felt that somehow I had to make it happen myself. When we went out after halftime, I talked one of the strikers into switching positions with me. I had always played midfield. My job was to bring the ball forward and pass it to the strikers; it was their job to score the goals. But now I said to him, "Give me ten minutes to be the striker. Ten minutes!"

It was only about a year since I had run from my first lion, and now the goalkeeper for the other team had become a lion to me. The soccer field had become the plains of northern Kenya, the great savanna. I was focused on the lion, and the lion was again looking at me right in the eye. I knew this was my chance. This time I was not going to turn back, to run away. I was thinking, "What can I do? How can I score a goal?" I was in a trance—an initiated warrior. I had spent so much time preparing to be a man. All the warrior songs were ringing in my ears.

And I did it! In 20 minutes I scored two goals—my first two goals ever. Of course, no one scores goals by himself. I owed a lot to my friend Kimutai. He was our right winger and one of the best players on the team. He fed me those shots.

So now the score was tied, two goals apiece. Only a

few minutes were left in the game. There was a lot of excitement, a lot of tension. We were at home, we were pumped up, momentum was on our side. We knew we could win. Our team had possession of the ball in our own half of the field. One of the defenders brought it forward toward midfield. It was clogged—the other team's midfielders were crowding him—but he found a small opening and put the ball through to Kimutai, who just took off down the right side. I knew how fast he was. I ran downfield and positioned myself in front of the goal, being careful not to get offside. Kimutai got past one defender, then a second, then a third. He put himself in a perfect position to cross the ball to me. I didn't have to do much: It was a perfect pass. I barely had to nudge it with my head to put it past the goalkeeper. Goal! I'd scored again.

We'd won the game, three goals to two, and I'd scored all three. And Kabarak had beaten the other school in three of the four events that day, so everyone was happy. It was a madhouse! Total jubilation. But as soon as the game was over, the president left without saying anything to us.

I DIDN'T HAVE MUCH TIME to think about the president. When I went back to my dormitory, I received word that my mother was ill. She'd gone out to get firewood with other women in some woods a few miles away from the village. They had spread out, and one of the other women was using an ax to chop the wood. The head of the ax—the metal part—was loose, and as she swung the ax, it came flying off. My mom wasn't paying attention—she was tying her wood into a bundle—and the ax head struck her right on the head. She was knocked out and bled a lot. Some of the beads she was wearing were driven into the wound. The women carried her back to the village. They dressed the wound with sheep fat and traditional herbs, which were supposed to kill infection and make the wound heal. But she was pretty sick.

Around eight o'clock that evening I was watching a movie in the dormitory with the other kids and worrying at the same time. Then, the president's bodyguards showed up and asked for me. The president wanted to see me, so I went over to his house, which was about a mile away. I'd been there before: Students were invited there for various functions. We'd eat lunch on the lawn, but we never saw the inside.

The president greeted me and took me to his study. We talked about the game and about my family back home. I told him about how we lived and about the drought and how we had lost a lot of cattle. It wasn't news to him: There was drought all over Kenya at that time. As I sat there, I started to relax. I'd been very tense at the beginning. Until then, the most powerful people I'd met were the headmaster of the school and the elders in my village, and there I was sitting with the most powerful man in Kenya. But as the conversation went on, I forgot I was talking to the president.

Eventually, I told him about my mom. He said, "Okay, get ready to leave in the morning. There's transport for you." He talked to the headmaster and arranged for me to take a leave. The next morning, there were two soldiers and a Land Rover waiting for me. Those guys had been told, "Take care of him. You're responsible if he doesn't come back!" They stuck to me tight, all the way. As I've said, the journey north was usually long and difficult for me. Now there I was, riding all the way in a government Land Rover with two bodyguards. When I showed up at home, my family thought I'd been arrested! I stayed for a few days with my mom—she was getting better—and then they drove me back to school.

So that was the beginning of my relationship with President Moi. But there was more to it. He is a good listener, and he doesn't forget a thing. I'd told him that there was a drought in the north and my family had lost a lot of cattle. They'd been selling cattle to pay my school fees, and between that and the drought, there weren't many left. Though I knew they'd make the sacrifice, I couldn't let them sell any more cows for me. I was going to have to drop out. And that's when the president stepped in. He became my sponsor and paid my fees for the rest of my time at Kabarak. And all because of a soccer game.

Chapter 10
America

The sun has risen from the west.
We hear nothing.
We fear no lion.

BACK WHEN I WAS A LITTLE KID in elementary school, I got the idea that someday I would go to America. Esther Anderson, one of the missionaries who ran the school, was from California. She would tell me, "Joseph, one day you'll go to school in America. You'll go to California." She told me that many times. And when I went home, I'd tell my mom I was going to America.

"America?" she'd say. "What is America?" She knew nothing about the place—and of course, neither did I. Nothing. I was a little nomadic kid who played in trees and hyena holes.

All the same, I'd tell her, "I'm going to go to America." And once something comes out of my mouth, it sticks. So all the time I was growing up, right on into high school, I had this ambition to go to the United States and finish my schooling there.

When the time came, I applied to American universities to take my degree. I took the SATs and English language examination. All the colleges I applied to accepted me, but none offered me a scholarship or any other financial aid. I didn't have the money—there weren't enough cows in Kenya to send me to school in America—so I thought, Well, I'll just have to change my plans. I'll go to the local university. I took my national examinations, and while I was waiting for the results to come in, I went to see President Moi.

"I need to do something before my results come and I go to college in Nairobi," I told him. "There's a bank in Marsabit, not far from my village. I'd like to work in the bank." It's really prestigious to work in a bank. Bankers are considered smart people, and they make a lot of money. I knew my family would be happy to know I had a bank job. So the president called the head of the bank and introduced me, and the next day I went down to Nairobi from Nakuru to meet him. I filled out some forms, and in a short time I had a job. I got a ride in a bank vehicle from Nairobi all the way home to Marsabit, and the president gave me some pocket money. I bought a new suit of clothes and some shoes.

So one day I was working at the bank when an American man came in with his family and a group of students. The students were all wearing T-shirts with St. Lawrence University printed on them. He was a big man with a beard. He said to me, "My students would like to change some American traveler's checks. Can you do this?" I asked for his passport and the checks and gave him the forms. While he was filling out the forms we talked.

It turned out later that Dennis Doyle, a man I knew in Nairobi, had sent the man from St. Lawrence University to see me while he was in Kenya doing fieldwork with his students. His name was Paul Robinson, and he was in Kenya as part of a program that provided scholarships to African students to study in the United States. The students in the group with him were part of the program. He asked me, "Have you thought of going to school in America?" I explained that I'd taken the test of English as a foreign language.

"I passed real well," I told him, "I got accepted to all these schools, but I have no money."

"Have you heard of St. Lawrence?" he asked me.

"Yeah," I said. "I see the T-shirts." A smart aleck.

But we went on talking, and when we finished he said, "Well, let me give you a call in a week or so." I was a little excited, but not much—I didn't think anything was going to come of it. But four days later he called and asked me if I could come down to Nairobi for an interview.

I took a truck down there. It was a cattle truck. I had to stand inside with the cows, and I had to help out. That's how it worked—you paid the driver a little money, but you also had to help out with the cows. The truck took forever, and the cows kept falling down. I helped pick them up. Sometimes they didn't want to get up—they're so stubborn. The only sure way to get a cow to stand is to take a piece of rubber and tie it over its nose and mouth. When it realizes that it can't breathe, it gets up. So that's how I got to Nairobi. I was a wreck by the time I got there: 330 miles, two days, standing in the truck with the cows going to the bathroom on my shoes, on my clothes. You can imagine how strong I smelled. That's how I had my interview: smelling of cows. Then I went back to the bank and waited. A few months later, I got a letter: I'd been accepted. I was going to St. Lawrence University, in Canton, New York, with a full scholarship.

No one I knew—except those missionaries—had ever been to America, and I knew nothing about it. I'd been told all sorts of stories.

"Don't eat with the wrong fork."

"Always watch your things—in New York, they'll steal them right from you."

"American women? Don't mess with them! They have little guns in their bags—small guns you can't see. And if you bother them, they just shoot you."

So there I was at Nairobi Airport, alone, with stories like these in my head, scared as a puppy. I'd been home to say good-bye to my mother and my brothers. My mother asked a lot of questions: "Are you afraid? Will you come back? Is America close to Nairobi?" Not that she had ever seen Nairobi. The Americans she knew were missionaries. She'd seen what they could do— drill wells, give medical treatment—and I think she thought I'd return like them. With my brothers, it was all man talk: the cattle, the weather, the grazing. They did not understand what I was doing, and they did not ask.

I rode a cattle truck from Marsabit to Nairobi, just the way I had for my interview. For two days before leaving, I literally couldn't eat—not a thing—I was so nervous. So by the time I checked in for my flight, I was very hungry. I was wearing a three-piece wool suit, with a collar and tie. I wanted to make the right impression. I had no idea how hot it was going to be in New York in August.

The first part of the journey was to London. I boarded the flight, and in the next seat there was an American man. I asked him where he was from. He told me, "Ohio." My English was terrible, but my geography was pretty good, and I knew where Ohio was, so we got along all right. An hour or two into the flight, they served a meal. I wanted to be careful not to embarrass myself in front of Americans. I certainly didn't want to offend my seatmate by using the wrong fork. And I wanted to be sure not to make any other mistake, like eating from the wrong side of the plate or starting with the entrée when I should have started with the salad, or something like that. The only way to get it exactly right, I thought, was to watch the man next to me, so when my food arrived, I sat reading a newspaper and sneaking glances to see what my neighbor was doing. He picked up his fork, so I picked up my fork. He pushed his food around a bit and picked at his salad, so I did the same.

Then he put his fork down. "*Aaah!* I don't like this airplane food," he said. "It's really bad."

So of course I did the same. "Me, too. It's very bad." And I was so hungry that I could have eaten my shoes!

Later, the flight attendant came by again and asked if we needed anything else. My neighbor told her, "No, I'm fine."

"How about you?" she asked me.

"No, I'm fine, too."

By then I was dying of hunger. But that's how it went, all the way to London. My neighbor didn't eat anything—just drank water. I didn't eat anything either, and I just got hungrier and hungrier. In London, I changed planes for the flight to New York. And do you know what? On the New York flight I was in the same seat, with the same guy next to me! By then I knew he wasn't going to touch his food. As soon as the plane took off I got a blanket, covered my head, and tried to sleep.

NAIROBI IS BIG, but it is nothing like New York. I looked down, and there was this huge city. At Kennedy Airport I was supposed to transfer to a plane to Syracuse. I'd written a letter to the YMCA in New York because they help international students with travel. Somebody was going to meet me at the plane, but I didn't realize the person couldn't come all the way to the gate. I stepped off the plane expecting somebody to be waiting right there, and when I didn't see anybody I panicked. So I followed everybody else, and I figured out that you have to go through immigration and pick up your luggage before you get to the meeting point. And eventually I found someone waiting for me—a young woman. I was so relieved, I gave her a hug—a big hug. I forgot all about those little guns!

She was supposed to take me from the international terminal to the domestic terminal so I could catch my flight to Syracuse. I had my things. I'd brought everything I owned: T-shirts, shorts—so worn out that people in America would just have thrown them away. Everything fit in two suitcases. I was still wearing my three-piece suit. I was hot, I was nervous, and I was hungry—all I'd had for about four days now was water. It was a terrible combination for someone in an unfamiliar place.

We started walking, and eventually my guide said, "Okay, Joseph. I have to leave you now. The terminal's not far; just go around here, take a left and a right and you'll be there." Now in my home, if somebody told me that, I'd think it was pretty far away. The village is just there? I'd think, probably four miles. And when somebody gives you directions, it's simple: "Climb the hill and the village is down below." There's no "left" and "right." "You go past the big tree." Simple—there's only one big tree. But this young woman had helped me and I didn't want to be a bother, so I thanked her and set off. I took two or three rights, whatever lefts came along—and in a few minutes I was completely lost. By the time I found my way to the right gate, I'd missed my flight.

It was about noon, and the next flight to Syracuse wasn't until four in the afternoon. So I sat down, pushed my suitcases under the chair, and waited for check-in. I was still nervous—every time someone came close to me, I'd cross my legs to hide my bags, afraid they might try to take them. Even old men and children.

I wanted to call the school to tell them I'd missed my flight. A student was going to meet me at the airport, and I wanted them to know I'd be late. I went to a pay phone, but I wasn't sure where to put the money or exactly how to make a long-distance call. Someone on the phone kept saying to me, "If you'd like to make a call, please hang up and dial again."

I didn't realize that it was a recording—I started arguing with the machine, saying, "I need to call this number. I don't understand. Why can't you help me?" This went on for a while. Finally, I saw a black man nearby. Back home, I'd been told, "When you see a black person, call him 'brother.'" So I asked him, "Brother, can you help me?"

"Are you from Africa, brother?" He could tell—my accent was so strong.

"Yes, I'm from Africa. Can you help me make this call?"

I explained my situation. He was sympathetic and he helped me get the call through to St. Lawrence, and I told them what had happened. Other people helped me out, too. A policeman watched my things while I went to the bathroom. I was in there for about five seconds—I went so quickly because I thought maybe he'd take them. Then finally check-in time came, and I was on my flight to Syracuse.

WHEN I ARRIVED, two female students were there to meet me. They had a car—it's about a three-hour drive from Syracuse to St. Lawrence—and we set off. It was a warm day, and they had the air conditioning turned all the way up. It was cold in the car, I was tired, and I hadn't eaten—I was almost sick. There I was, someone who'd learned to survive out in the open with the cattle back home, who'd learned to go without food and water all day—and I was helpless. I couldn't do anything. I started shaking.

One of the women asked me, "Joseph! Are you okay? Did you eat?"

I said, "No."

"Are you hungry?"

"No." Because back home, a warrior never accepts food from a woman. It goes against tradition; if a woman asks if you're hungry and you say yes, it makes you appear weak. It's unacceptable. So I said, "No, I'm fine."

"Are you cold?"

"No. I'm fine, really." This happened several times. They asked me, "Are you sure you don't want to eat?" and I kept telling them, "No, it's fine." I knew it was a long drive; I thought that if I could just go to sleep until the next day, I'd be able to figure out what to do. But finally I couldn't take it anymore. Part of me was acting on tradition; part of me was worried about embarrassing myself and eating the wrong way—and part of me was thinking, I hope they ask me just one more time. I guess I realized that the state of New York wasn't going to look down on me if I accepted the offer of a meal.

The opportunity came at McDonald's. By then it was about ten o'clock in the evening. "Joseph, we're stopping at McDonald's here. Are you sure you're not hungry?"

I asked, "Are there any chips?" I didn't know what chips were called in the United States, but one of the women had been to Europe and she knew.

"French fries?"

"Potatoes—chips. Yes!"

They were so excited. They bought me a big burger and a big order of french fries, and I felt a lot better. And that was my introduction to America—McDonald's.

Chapter 11
A Warrior in Two Worlds

The lion ate my favorite cow,
That gave the most milk.
The warriors of the mountain,
The mountains of grass and streams,
And the life of our people—
That lion is no more.

WHEN I TELL MY MOM about the sun—how it doesn't move—she thinks I'm crazy. I tell her, "Mom, the sun is fixed. It's the Earth that moves around the sun."

She says, "OK, Son. I'm putting this rock here. Let's see if it's going to move before tomorrow." She just doesn't understand it. If I ask her what she thinks happens, she says, "Well, Son. I think the sun goes down, goes all the way underground, and rises up on the other side of the country."

"And how about the stars?"

"Well, the stars—during the day, they go out and graze, like the cows do. So you don't see them. At night, they come home and sleep, and we see them up there."

That's all she knows. For her, there's just nature. Bring science, bring technology to her, and she'll never really get it. If there's an eclipse of the moon, she thinks that we did something wrong, and she prays. When I'm home and staying with her in her hut, I'll sometimes hear her get up in the night and pray: "Thanks for bringing my son home. Thanks for the things you've done for me. And bring the moon back!"

I tell her, "Mom, when I come home, I fly here." She has no idea where America is. She knows it's far away, that's all. She'd never get in a plane. She sees them up there, but they don't mean anything to her. So I tell her, "My plane leaves at 6:30 in the morning, when you take the cows out. You go the whole day, and the cows come home, and I'm still up in the air. And you sleep, and I'm still traveling, and the next day when you take the cows out again is when I reach America."

She says, "All that time, you're up there?"

"Yes."

"And you eat and move around in the plane?"

"Yes."

And she says, "Son, I don't believe it. But I trust you. I trust what you're telling me."

The thing is, I spent very little time with my mother when I was growing up. I was away at boarding schools from the age of six, and when I wasn't at school I was usually at cattle camp with my brothers and the other men. I was learning how a boy is supposed to live, learning our traditions, how to be brave, how to protect the cattle—and not to involve myself too much with women. That's our culture. I'd see my mother for perhaps ten days a year. So now I make it a point to spend time with her. I go home to Kenya during the school vacations, and I spend two or three weeks with her, telling her what I'm doing and finding out from her about life at home.

Whenever I go home, I bring her a present— usually some cloth. It's not very much: As I told you, she doesn't have many possessions, she doesn't live like that. After college, I became a teacher in McLean, Virginia, at The Langley School. A teacher doesn't make a lot of money, but I always saved what I could. I wanted to do something more for my mom. At the end of my second year teaching, I took a group of students and parents to Kenya during the summer vacation. They saw where I came from, what kind of life I'd lived as a child, the kind of huts we lived in. I told them, "This is how my mother lives. She lives in a hut like this." And I was thinking about what I could do for her.

At the end of the trip, the group gave me some money, to help me and to say thanks. I took that money, put it in an envelope, wrapped it tight with a rubber band, and stuffed it away at the bottom of my bag. I didn't even look at it—I thought, if I see it, I'm going to want to spend it. I knew I wanted to do something special for my mom. So I went home, and with Lmatarion and a friend and some soldiers I knew, I went up to an area near the Ethiopian border where there are a lot of cows. With the group's money and the money I had been saving, I bought my mom some cattle.

The cows up there were a good breed. They were more drought resistant and gave more milk than our cows. I thought that they would be the perfect present for my mom—not only for her, but for the whole community. There would be more milk for everybody, and the new cattle would improve our breeding stock. So we went up there and bought the cows. We arranged for transportation, then we drove home. I never said a word to my mom, so she wasn't expecting anything.

The cows arrived about a week later. I made sure that they were brought to the village early in the morning.

Mornings are regarded as a blessing. As the sun was coming up, I brought the cows into the kraal, one by one, eight of them. I said to my mom, "This is a gift for you. What you've done for me has been incredible. You've supported me my whole life, through all the tough decisions to allow me to stay in school. When people wanted me to drop out, you made me stay. So this is your gift. Come and see your cows." She couldn't believe it! She couldn't say a word. She just went and looked at them, touched them.

It was time for the cattle to go out and graze, so the new cows went out with the rest of the herd. When they came back that evening, Mom went out and looked at them again, and that night she woke up many times to go out to be with them. What she was doing was naming them. In the morning, she took me out and told me their names—"This is so-and-so, this is so-and-so, this is so-and-so." She was very happy. I knew it was going to make her happy, but I didn't know how happy. And now the kids in the village are saying, "I'll go to school to buy cows for my mom, like Lekuton did." It's been very good.

Afterword

More About Joseph Lemasolai Lekuton
and the Ariaal People
BY HERMAN VIOLA

JOSEPH LEMASOLAI LEKUTON is a remarkable man, one I am privileged to call my friend. Half the year Joseph is a social studies teacher at The Langley School, a prestigious private school near Washington, D.C. The other half he is a Maasai warrior in northern Kenya following the traditional nomadic cattle-herding culture of his people. He recently completed a master's degree in international education policy at Harvard University and intends to use his skills to improve the lives of the traditional nomadic peoples of East Africa, whose proud and durable way of life is under increasing stress from the pressures of modern society.

Upon graduating from St. Lawrence University, Joseph decided that he wanted to teach in American schools for a few years. Uncertain how to go about

finding a job, he filed his résumé with a teacher place-
ment service and hoped for the best. The first phone call
of many that he eventually received came from Betty
Brown, at that time the headmistress of The Langley
School in McLean, Virginia. The Langley School was
founded in 1947 as a cooperative school and is now one
of the premier private educational institutions in the
region. Betty had looked at Joseph's résumé and liked
what she saw.

"When I looked at his résumé, I knew he was a very
unusual person who had a lot he could contribute from
his own culture to the students at The Langley School,"
she recalls. "I thought any young man whose people
would put up their livelihood, their cattle, to send him
to school certainly had their absolute endorsement of
him, yet, the fact that he was bright enough to get a
scholarship so he did not need the cattle spoke well of
his ability. I passed around his résumé at a faculty
retreat, and one of the teachers sent me a note saying,
'Are you crazy?' I said, 'Yes, a little bit, but this is one
young man I want to meet.'"

Upon returning from the retreat, Betty asked
Joseph to visit Langley for an interview. He was somewhat hesitant because of her Southern accent (he had
been warned that the American South was no place for

an ambitious black man), but she told him that Washington, D.C., was an interesting and welcoming city, that Langley was a super school. She convinced him to come down and take a look.

"When I met him I was even more impressed," Betty said. "I realized he was a person between two cultures, but I saw him as a global citizen. He is one of only two teachers in my career—and I have probably interviewed over a thousand teaching applicants—to whom I offered a contract on the spot. We really wanted him. He is very kind, a fine human being as well as a real scholar. Moreover, he has a wonderful attitude and outlook on life. At any school you have teachers who come in and mumble and complain, but when they run into Joseph, they leave with a little lilt in their step. They're almost skipping after they see him. 'What do you say?' I will ask him. 'I tell them to look at the sky, to see what a beautiful day it is.' Joseph sees the beauty of everything around him. He makes people who are miserable and complaining happy—not by saying forget it, or snap out of it, but by saying something that lets people see what a wonderful world it is. He tells everyone you can overcome any hardship and meet any challenge, and Joseph has certainly done that. It is a sort of contagious quality. No one ever wants to complain around Joseph because he always puts a positive spin on things. And the students love him as well. He comes from such a different background than our kids, yet they bond with him immediately. He has such a winning smile. He turned out absolutely wonderful."

TO UNDERSTAND JOSEPH, it is first necessary to understand the Ariaal people, whose home is the savanna of northern Kenya. Their livelihood relies upon livestock, mainly cattle, but also goats, sheep, camels, and donkeys. The Ariaal are a small, Maa-speaking group, whose population is estimated to be about 100,000, but an accurate census is difficult to obtain because, as Joseph explains, it is considered improper in his culture to count people.

The Ariaal homeland is quite dry, mostly arid plains and semi-deserts, consisting of lowlands and highlands. The higher areas are cooler and wetter than the lowlands. Lowland temperatures are often near 100 degrees Fahrenheit, and even in the best of times rain may not fall for months. Lacking the rainfall necessary to grow crops, the Ariaal must rely for survival upon their vast herds of livestock, which can be moved from pasture to pasture as season, rainfall, and other factors dictate.

Ariaal settlements usually consist of a few families. A thorny fence called a *boma* made of acacia branches protects their livestock at night. Each family has its own gate into the compound, and each married woman in the compound has her own house. The Ariaal are polygamous, which means a man can have more than one wife. Women own their houses, which they build with cow dung plastered over a wooden frame. Husbands sleep in the houses of their wives.

Ariaal society revolves around age and gender. Men and women behave according to long established principles based on age. Males, for example, belong to an age-set determined by the date of their circumcision, which marks their initiation into manhood. Men of an age set may have been born a dozen or more years apart, but in Ariaal society they are considered the same age and, like fraternity brothers, they will be friends for life. The most recently circumcised males form an *Ilmurran*, essentially a brotherhood of warriors who are responsible for protecting the community and its livestock. Warriors live separately from the other villagers, are not allowed to marry or eat any food seen or offered by a woman, and spend their free time making themselves glamorous by wearing long braids powdered with red ochre and by practicing their singing and dancing skills.

The tenure of each Ilmurran is determined by when the next group of males is circumcised, usually after 14 or 15 years. Once that occurs, the men of the former Ilmurran cut off their braids, marry, and enter the fraternity of elders, the most powerful group in the society.

The life of Ariaal women is less regulated. Girls usually marry as teenagers and are at least 15 years younger than their husbands. A woman's prestige rises as she matures and has children, especially when she has sons who become warriors. A woman identifies herself with her husband's family after marriage. Names and property such as livestock are only passed from father to son. Although a woman cannot inherit property from her father, she often receives gifts of livestock that she brings to the marriage. After marriage, a girl's mother gives her gourds and other items she needs for her household. These and the house she builds belong only to her.

Daily life revolves around the care of the livestock. Because the animals must be taken out to pasture every single day, families rise before dawn. Mothers relight the cooking fires and prepare a simple breakfast of tea and porridge. The children then take the animals out to assigned pastures. The workday does not end until dusk, when the cows return and are milked. The evenings are spent in conversation, telling stories, and often in singing and dancing. Because their day begins at dawn, Ariaal families usually retire early to sleep.

Children do much of the herding. Boys and girls as young as five or six take the little animals—calves, sheep, and goats—to grazing areas near their homes, learning early to become responsible, productive members of society.

The warriors have responsibility for the mature animals. Often they have to take the community herds long distances to find adequate grass and water. Sometimes, during the dry season or in periods of severe drought, they must establish cattle camps far from the villages and remain away from home for weeks at a time. On these occasions older boys and girls will also be sent to the camps to help with the chores and give the warriors a break in the routine. It was at one of these camps that Joseph—as a young warrior—had his first confrontation with a lion.

Ariaal food comes from their livestock. Milk is the staple of the diet. It is drunk fresh or after it has fermented a few days, becoming a form of yogurt or cottage cheese. Milk is stored in a calabash, a type of gourd that is cleaned with burning sticks, which gives the milk a unique taste.

Meat is not eaten very often. Although the Ariaal

have a great many cows, goats, and sheep, they are too valuable to be slaughtered for food. Animals are killed only for special occasions and certain ceremonies. Otherwise they are traded for grain, sugar, tea, cloth, and other necessities, sold, or kept for breeding purposes. Animal blood, on the other hand, is an important part of the diet. Blood can be drunk plain, mixed with milk, or cooked into porridge.

Like the other pastoralists of Kenya, the Ariaal are threatened by modern society. Towns and wildlife preserves now occupy some of their prime grazing lands; roads bring unwelcome visitors and change, and the government encourages nomads to give up herding and settle into towns, where they become dependent on government assistance to survive.

Those groups that continue to cling to their traditional way of life are such a small minority in Kenya that they find themselves isolated and unprotected even by their own government.

I MET JOSEPH IN 1994, when he joined the faculty of The Langley School, where my wife, Susan, administers the Pat Bush Library. I had spent much of my career at the Smithsonian Institution as a historian, working with the tribal peoples of North America, so Susan knew I would enjoy meeting her new colleague, who was a tribal person from Africa.

How right she was! Joseph is a fabulous storyteller. From our first conversation at dinner one night at our home, I was mesmerized by his stories and was eager to help him tell them to a larger audience. As I explained what I had in mind, Joseph willingly agreed to the idea, insisting only that we write the story for young people rather than for adults. He wants to use his life as an example to let kids know that they can overcome whatever obstacles appear in their path as long as they pick a goal and do their best.

During the writing of this book, my wife and I accompanied Joseph to Kenya one summer. He led us on a typical tourist safari with two other couples from the Washington, D.C., area. It was a profound experience in many ways. One was in discovering just how far Joseph had come from the African savanna, not in distance but in personal achievement. Fellow Africans were incredulous at the thought that a black man, especially an Ariaal, was in charge of a group of white Americans. Indeed, his people are at the bottom stratum of Kenyan society. At the four-star hotels in the Masai Mara, and in other tourist hotels in the nomadic inhabited areas, the higher level employees—waiters, hostesses, and managers, for example—are members of Kenya's dominant tribes. If the Maasai are employed at all, it is in menial jobs, such as cleaning or chasing the monkeys out of the eating areas with their slingshots.

Such expectations are so ingrained that native Kenyans and tourists alike are startled when they meet a cattle herder who is fluent in English. English is one of the official languages of Kenya but rarely penetrates remote areas.

JOSEPH LOVES TO TELL the following story about such an encounter that took place one summer while he was a college student.

"When I go home," he explains, "I sometimes dress traditionally—my beads, my spear, my club. One day my brother, my cousin, and I took our cows into the national forest for water. When we were crossing the road that separates communal land from the park, we met a van with an African driver and about eight American tourists. They saw us and stopped.

"They yelled '*Jambo,* jambo, jambo!—Hello, hello, hello!' And they wanted to take our pictures. But, it is illegal in Kenya to take native people's pictures without their permission, and all tourists are informed of this law. Despite this their driver, who dressed like someone from the city, said, 'Go ahead. You take a picture of these guys, but pretend you're photographing the national park and the woods.' So they came piling out their van, yelling 'Jambo, Jambo Kenya!' I said, 'Jambo America!'

"Of course they had no idea that I could speak or understand English. They came close to us to take pictures but pretended they were only looking at us with their binoculars. I decided it might be funny to give them a little scare.

"When one of them finished focusing his camera and was about to hit the button, I said, softly, 'Hey, wait a minute.' They all looked up. They were so surprised. They were more than surprised. They didn't know whether this remark came from me or someone in their party, so the guy started focusing again. This time I said in a gruff voice, 'Hey, what part of what I said didn't you understand? I said wait a minute!' By this time, the van driver figured out what was happening and took off. He ran to the van, jumped in, and locked the door.

"When I saw the driver take off, I said to my brother and cousin, 'What a silly man. Why don't you go and scare him a bit.' So they went over to the van and starting breathing heavily, pressing their faces against the windows, and singing and waving their spears and clubs.

"The tourists were shocked. I said, 'Okay, folks, you broke the rules. In America when you break the law, you pay the price. The same thing in Kenya.'

"Now they were beginning to panic. They didn't realize I was just fooling around with them.

"'Where are you from?' one of them asked.

"'Where I'm from is not really the issue,' I said. 'The issue is that one of the first things you are told when you come here is not to take pictures of the natives without their permission, so don't give me that stuff about where I'm from.'

"That did it. They began pleading with me, pleading. These guys were so scared. The Americans must have asked me 50 times, 'Where are you from? Where did you learn English?'

"The joke had gone far enough. It was so hard for me to keep from laughing. Finally, a kind-looking woman about my mother's age asked me where I went to school. That did it for me. I said, 'I go to school in America. Upstate New York.' As soon as I said that, one of the tourists shouted, 'Buffalo! Buffalo! I'm from Buffalo!'

"Now I started smiling. 'You know, folks, you ought to obey the rules of our country. You're taking pictures of my family without asking. If you want pictures, you can take them, but next time, please ask.'

"By now the van driver was so scared he was underneath the van's seat. So I called my cousin and brother back to pose for pictures with the nice people.

"My aim was to make an impression. When those tourists got back home and looked at their pictures, maybe they would remember that someone might look ignorant and primitive, but that is no reason to try to take advantage of him."

WHILE AT ST. LAWRENCE UNIVERSITY and at The Langley School, Joseph has returned to Kenya during each school vacation. Every summer he takes a group of students to Kenya to introduce them to his people. The trips serve a dual purpose: to educate Americans about Africa and to encourage them to return the favor by providing some educational resources and other material support to the Ariaal. Thanks to Joseph and the Langley parents, his mother's village and the villages nearby now have clean running water, a modern school and dormitory, computers, and other benefits. As Joseph says, "It has been good."

Acknowledgements

I would like to thank the following:

Herman and Susan Viola, whose guidance and direction were instrumental in telling my story. Without them, I would not have even tried to write this book. Susan, thanks for introducing me to Herman.

Simon Boughton, for helping get this book off the ground.

National Geographic, where I am especially grateful to Nancy Laties Feresten, who saw promise in my book and agreed to be my editor and publisher.

The former President of Kenya, Daniel arap Moi, and Kabarak high school for giving me a chance to stay in school after a severe drought left my family without enough cattle to pay my school fees.

My family and friends, Nkasiko, Sophia, Lonunu, Ntachamwa, Naripukule, Paraikon, Ngoliong, Lmatarion, Mpirison, Lekeyon, Letom, Ntelelek, Ldirait, Lengima, Ntarkyan, Sapian, Mpenoi, Reitanoi, Ngoronkwe, Loroklala, Mpaari, Matin, Kennedi, Ltasayon, Ntayai, Ltalemon, Ltalipen, Lterewa, Mugunten, Rita, Jeiso, Kargiya, Iltangalan, Lumba, Nkikor, Moluaya, Lmariaton, Mardadi, Nkariasan, Lekorole, Simba, Lteshon, Lowankiya, Lmeingach, Ltaramatwa, Ngoley, Lekerle, Ndirangu, Chapa, and many more in all the villages, and cattle camps of Northern Kenya. The elders (men and women) of the Karare, Logologo, Kamboe, Laisamis, Ngurnit, Ndikir, Merelle, Ilaut, Korr, Kargi, Mt. Kulal, Loyangalani, Namarei, Songa, Kituruni, HulaHula, and South Horr villages who helped me to grow up and to love my culture.

My good friend in Kenya, Colonel Philip Laibon Lepakiyo, and his family.

Kathleen Colson and her family, Doug, Will, Ellie, Daniel, for their love and friendship, and the Longtrail School in Dorset, Vermont.

My Harvard friends, Holly Zimmerman, Mei Mei Peng, Eric Waldo, Patricia Cerqueira, Rachel Garver, David Willard, Brian Finn, Jason Carpenter, and LeAnna Marr, who gave me additional support.

My Harvard professors, Kai Ming Cheng, Sue Grant Lewis, Claudia Bach, Mitra Shavirini, and Joe Kalt for giving me the power of knowledge.

Paul Robinson, Howard Brown, Dennis Doyle, Bruce and Anne Benedict, and Patti McGill Peterson for giving me the chance to come to St. Lawrence University, and David Vrooman and Ahmed Samatar for their skillful pedagogy.

Special thanks to Doris Cottam and the entire Langley School students, faculty, parents, and staff who gave me the support I need.

The following Langley families for opening up their homes, and their friendships: the Kanters, Laysons, Gorells, Finns, Shermans, Smiths, Carrs, Barths, Mitches, Hudeceks, Cowans, Millers, Frenches, Lefraks, Hutchins, Warens, Cases, Pecaros, Browns, Gemmels, Crumpekers, Grooms, Hunts, Riedys, Elliots, Martins, Hrens, Silvanos, Chuzis, Rohrbachs, Leedoms, Holmers, Minors, Queenans, Taylors, Weisses, Gubermans, Gleasons, Klunders, Raneses, Pascals, Venners, Feldmans, Hinderdaels, Magruders, Freedmans, Feehans, Solomons, Stones, Wilkins, DiGiammarinos, Wallaces, Hayeses, Breyers, Doyles, Earp, Fifers, Foust, Johnsons, Hellers, Magnussons, Narangs, O'Connells, Rosens, Serotas, Sunshines, and many more. You have all been there for me when I needed you. Thank you.

Jill Rademacher for teaching me the meaning of getting organized, and for always being there when I needed her friendship.

The Wolfes and the Beers for their continued support of my dream.

Nomadic Kenya Children Education Fund for their education support.

Loldapash and Mark Poole of the Maasai Environmental Resource Coalition for giving the Maasai people a voice.

Ricki Kanter and her family for their friendship and for planning my trip to Boston, and more.

Andrew Dabalen and family for his wise advice   always.

Randy Odeneal and Sue Falk for their special friendship and for the confidence they have in me.

Ashley Lefrak and her family for taking pictures for my book, and—with the Hutchins and other Langley families—for giving Mantaine Minis a new heart. She is now playing with other little Maasai girls in the African savanna.

The Welters—Tony, Bea, Bryant, and Andrew—for always making me feel a part of their family, for realizing what dreams I have, and for striving to help me achieve them, including giving the gift of life (water) to thousands of nomads in Northern Kenya, and for their constant encouragement, which makes me a better person. Thank you very much.

It is impossible to thank all the individuals that are part of my life or who in one way or another assisted in the preparation of this book, and I apologize for those I forgot. Your absence in print does not represent an absence of your influence.

A Note from the Author

IN NOMADIC KENYA, where I grew up, most children are forced to chose between family duties and an education. They walk miles to find drinking water and have limited access to proper medical care. It is my sincere hope and ambition that all nomadic children have the opportunity to further their educations and grow up to strengthen my people, my country, and the world. If you would like to help further my dream, here are some organizations to contact.

The Nomadic Kenyan Children's Educational Fund (NKCEF) was founded to help provide nomadic Kenyan children a solid educational foundation. NKCEF has established the Joseph Lekuton Scholarship Program to award scholarships to nomadic students. To learn more about NKCEF visit http://www.nkcef.org.

The Maasai Environmental Resource Coalition (MERC) supports community-based development projects in Maasai communities throughout Kenya and Tanzania. MERC programs help to preserve the Maasai culture, increase access to educational and economic opportunities, and protect the traditional land rights of the Maasai people. To learn more about MERC visit http://www.maasaierc.org/specialprojects.html.

One of the world's largest nonprofit scientific and educational organizations, the National Geographic Society was founded in 1888 "for the increase and diffusion of geographic knowledge." Fulfilling this mission, the Society educates and inspires millions every day through its magazines, books, television programs, videos, maps and atlases, research grants, the National Geographic Bee, teacher workshops, and innovative classroom materials. The Society is supported through membership dues, charitable gifts, and income from the sale of its educational products. This support is vital to National Geographic's mission to increase global understanding and promote conservation of our planet through exploration, research, and education.

For more information, please call
1-800-NGS-LINE (647-5463) or write to the following address:
National Geographic Society
1145 17th Street N.W.
Washington, D.C. 20036-4688 U.S.A.
Visit the Society's Web site: www.nationalgeographic.com

AGNES DE MILLE

Rachel Gaskill

rosen
central™

The Rosen Publishing Group, Inc., New York

Published in 2006 by The Rosen Publishing Group, Inc.
29 East 21st Street, New York, NY 10010

Library of Congress Cataloging-in-Publication Data

Gaskill, Rachel.
Agnes de Mille / Rachel Gaskill.—1st ed.
    p. cm. — (The library of American choreographers)
Includes bibliographical references and index.
ISBN 1-4042-0444-X (lib. bdg.)
ISBN 1-4042-0645-0 (pbk. bdg.)
1. De Mille, Agnes—Juvenile literature. 2. Choreographers—United
States—Biography—Juvenile literature.
I. Title. II. Series.
GV1785.D36G37 2006
792.8'092—dc22
                                            2004029468
Manufactured in the United States of America

On the Cover: Inset: Agnes de Mille in 1952. Background: The original
company performs in the 1943 production of *Oklahoma!*, choreographed
by Agnes de Mille.

Contents

Introduction   4

1 The Early Years in
      New York City   6

2 The Struggle to Begin
      Dance Training   14

3 The World Takes Notice   22

4 De Mille's Lasting Legacy   34

Glossary   44

For More Information   45

For Further Reading   46

Bibliography   46

Index   47

Introduction

In New York City in 1928, young Agnes de Mille was at another of her many dance auditions, this one for one of the toughest European ballet company managers. For the audition, Agnes performed four dances. Following her performance, the manager explained that she was lacking the right look and style and was not meant for the theater. As de Mille recounts in her autobiography *Dance to the Piper* (1952), "Mother entered without one word and, putting both arms around me, drew my head down on her shoulder. 'My father used to say,' she spoke quietly, 'that a way would become apparent as we go along. In the end a door always opens.'" These proved to be very powerful and prophetic words, for fifteen years later a door would indeed open.

As stated in *Broadway, the Golden Years*, "When Agnes de Mille created *Oklahoma!* in 1943, she changed the nature of the American

The original Broadway theater poster for the premier 1943 production of Rodgers and Hammerstein's *Oklahoma!* appears at right. Agnes de Mille provided the choreography for this wildly popular and innovative musical.

musical." Before that, dance hadn't played a major role in the story line of musicals. Agnes put dance at the center of musical comedy by making it an important part of the development of the story. The attention and importance that was traditionally reserved for stars, directors, and producers were now given to choreographers as well. She paved the way for the choreographer-director whose name would now appear on the marquee along with the production's other credits. Having introduced dance to storytelling on Broadway, de Mille started a trend, and for a decade mini-ballets were often featured in many Broadway musicals.

1 The Early Years in New York City

Agnes de Mille was born on September 18, 1905, to William and Anna de Mille. At that time, they were living on 118th Street in Harlem, in New York City. A few years later her sister, Margaret, was born.

Agnes loved her father very much. He was a major influence in her life. It was William de Mille who first introduced her to theater. Both he and her paternal grandfather were successful playwrights. Since her father was a playwright, Agnes was determined to be an actress. In her autobiography *Dance to the Piper*, she describes how, as a child, she practiced her acting every night in bed. She would re-create dreadful scenes where she was screaming and crying. She also practiced her own stretches so that when she arrived in Hollywood, she would be ready for anything physically demanded of her.

In *Dance to the Piper*, de Mille describes her shift away from acting: "It was only after

This family photograph shows Agnes de Mille as a young girl. She was born on September 18, 1905, on West 118th Street in Harlem, New York. When she was ten, her family moved to Hollywood, California, to pursue opportunities in the film industry. Agnes began attending the Hollywood School for Girls, a private performing arts school.

seeing a matinee performance of Adeline Genée, dainty, doll-like and impeccable, that I altered my choice of vocation. I declared on coming home that henceforth I would be a ballet dancer." Her parents did not approve of her wanting to become a dancer. She wasn't allowed to take dance lessons, but her mother encouraged her to improvise nightly while she provided the music to accompany her. This became an evening routine, and sometimes she was permitted to dance for dinner guests.

Uncle Cecil B. DeMille

Agnes's uncle, Cecil B. DeMille (he changed the "d" in his last name to a capital), was also in the theater business. He had a rocky start in New York as an actor and play-wright. He also suffered many failed business ventures. But DeMille did not get discouraged. He became involved in a new plan to start a motion picture company in Flagstaff, Arizona. He asked his brother, William (Agnes's father), to invest five thousand dollars. Given DeMille's past business failures, his brother refused.

Instead, DeMille joined with partners Jesse Lasky and Sam Goldfish (later Goldwyn) and in 1913 headed west. Once in Hollywood, he started producing successful feature (full-length) films. Most movies during that time were not feature length, but were instead five- to ten-minute silent short films. DeMille made himself director general of the Lasky Company. This company would later be known as Paramount Pictures. According to *Broadway, the Golden Years*, Cecil B. DeMille enjoyed one of the most successful careers in Hollywood history and became one of the industry's most powerful figures. In *Dance to the Piper*, de Mille states that her uncle Cecil is one of the most remarkable men she has ever known. One of the strongest forces in her life was her desire to fit into the mold of what he defined as a star.

Meanwhile, back home in New York, Agnes's

Agnes de Mille's uncle, Cecil B. DeMille, was a famous and successful Hollywood director, producer, and screenwriter. Agnes's father moved the family to Hollywood in order to join his brother in the film business. In this circa 1934 photo, he appears with his daughter, Kathryn (*right*), and his niece, Agnes (*left*). At this time, Kathryn was working in a movie with Mae West entitled *It Ain't No Sin*, while Agnes was hired as a dancer for her uncle's latest film, *Cleopatra*.

father had just experienced his first failure with a play. His brother Cecil really wanted him to come to Hollywood. The film business was growing very quickly, and DeMille felt his brother would find great writing opportunities there. So he persuaded him to come out and give it a try. In 1915, Agnes, her mother, Anna, and her sister, Margaret, left New York City and joined the brothers in Hollywood.

Hollywood

Ten-year-old Agnes was thrilled to be going to Hollywood! She was hopeful that she would someday be allowed to act in movies. Hollywood was much different than she expected.

Its landscape was not nearly as exciting or beautiful as the western lands they had traveled through by train. Hollywood at that time was mostly woodlands. Cowboys rode their horses on dirt roads that crossed the town's one paved street. Once the de Milles arrived, they spent the first few nights with Uncle Cecil. Shortly after, Agnes's mother found them a house of their own. It was at the foot of a hill bordering the woods.

Agnes was hoping for a week or two of free time to get settled in California, but her mother had other plans. She found a school for Agnes and Margaret within two days. Classes in the Hollywood School for Girls

A fourteen-year-old Agnes de Mille (*right*) and her sister, Margaret, aged eleven, play act in costume in the garden of their Hollywood home.

were held outside in a garden. The class Agnes enjoyed most was pantomime, where they used only silent actions and facial expressions to tell a complete story. The school also offered dance classes, but her mother didn't allow Agnes to take any. She didn't want Agnes to ruin her natural talent. So Agnes watched the other girls learning dances based on the choreography of Ruth St. Denis and Isadora Duncan, two pioneers in modern dance.

Agnes's mother would occasionally take the girls to see dance concerts. When Agnes was thirteen, she saw Anna Pavlova dance. Pavlova was a famous ballerina from Russia. Seeing Pavlova dance had an enormous impact on her. Agnes was amazed by Pavlova's passion for dance. From then on, she knew she had to dance. Agnes begged her parents again for lessons, but they still refused. Shortly after seeing the dance concert, she announced to her neighborhood friends that they would put on their own dance concert in the backyard. Even though none of them had taken any formal dance lessons, they were not discouraged. They wrote a program on paper and had Agnes's mother create costumes for them. They created many improvisational dances, and some dances were based on the concerts Agnes had seen.

Agnes's Big Break

Much to Agnes's dismay, her parents continued to refuse to give her formal dance lessons. Her father didn't want her to have a career in any form of theater, and her mother was still worried the formal lessons would ruin her natural creative talent. Everything Agnes learned about dance,

Anna Pavlova

Anna Pavlova was the most famous female dancer in the world in the early twentieth century. She was the principal ballerina of her own company, and she toured the world introducing many people to classical ballet. She is known for her powerful stage presence. Her performances created an interest in ballet and inspired young people to pursue careers in dance.

Russian ballerina Anna Pavlova dances the title role in *The Dying Swan* in this circa 1910 photograph. She endured a childhood of poor health and frailty to become the most famous and talented ballet dancer of her time.

she learned by reading and looking at magazines. She would even create scrapbooks by cutting out magazine photographs of famous dancers.

Agnes finally received her lucky break when her sister, Margaret, developed trouble with the arches in her feet. The doctor recommended that she take ballet as a form of physical therapy. Agnes's mother was always very fair with her children, so if Margaret would be taking ballet then so, too, would Agnes.

The Struggle to Begin Dance Training

2

Agnes was thirteen when she started taking ballet lessons at the Theodore Kosloff School of Imperial Russian Ballet in Hollywood. Theodore Kosloff had been trained at Moscow's Imperial Theatre school and had gone on to become a member of the Russian impresario Sergei Diaghilev's company, the Ballets Russes in Paris. Kosloff eventually returned to the United States and began his own company. This company toured the states and ended up in Hollywood, where Kosloff was hired by Cecil DeMille's scouts to do some work on DeMille's latest film. Kosloff stayed in Hollywood, where he settled down with his wife and child and continued to act while developing his dance school. As a courtesy to Uncle Cecil, he agreed to take Agnes and Margaret on as pupils free of charge.

In *Dance to the Piper*, de Mille describes her first audition: "Kosloff himself put me through the test. He did not say how talented

I was or how naturally graceful. He said my knees were weak, my spine curved, that I was heavy for my age and had 'no juice.'" Agnes later learned that meant that her muscles were stubborn and not willing to change easily. Kosloff also said she was a bit old to start training. Agnes wasn't quite sure how to respond or feel. She was hurt by the criticism but also so thrilled to finally be receiving professional help.

Struggle and Discouragement

As much as Agnes was thrilled to finally be taking dance classes, it was not at all easy. At times she found it very frustrating and difficult. As hard as ballet technique is to master and perform, it is meant to appear easy, graceful, and light. She also struggled with her body image. She didn't have a classical ballet body, which is typically long and lean. Agnes was short (as an adult she was only 5 feet 1 [1.5 meters]) with wide hips and short arms and legs. However, she soon found that her endurance was one of her greatest assets, as was her determination.

The other ballet students had class every day, but Agnes was only allowed one forty-five-minute private lesson a week and one sixty-minute class lesson a week. In between classes she would

Agnes de Mille (*above*) did not fit the traditional mold of the ballerina. Her body and feet were tiny, yet she was heavier than most other dancers. She was also older and less experienced than most ballerinas in her classes. One of her remedies for these shortcomings was to design dances for herself. This led her to choreography, where her true talent lay.

practice at home in her mother's bathroom, where her mother had put in a small ballet barre for her. Agnes did not like practicing there. She did not like working alone without a teacher's eyes to correct her. In addition, the floor was slippery and there was no mirror.

In *Dance to the Piper*, de Mille describes her frustration with her limited practice time and resulting lack of skill: "The plain truth is I was the worst pupil in the class. Having grown into adolescence feeling that I was remarkably gifted and destined to be great, I now found I could not hold my own with any of the girls standing on the floor beside me." For all the hardships, though, she still loved ballet and loved being in class.

Ultimately, the lack of regular dance classes led to great frustration. Agnes began to dread her lonely practice in her mother's bathroom with no music and proper equipment. She realized that by taking a class only twice a week she was not progressing as the other girls were. In *Dance to the Piper*, she states, "By the time I got through high school, dancing meant exhaustion and little else." Agnes's father finally began to see the struggle Agnes was having keeping up in dance. He sat her down and told her that she should either give dancing 100 percent or forget about it and move on. Finally, he had reached a point where he would support her decision if she chose dance.

All the years of his disapproval had taken their toll, however, and her lack of intensive practice had disheartened her. As she says in *Dance to the Piper*, "One morning toward the end of summer I walked into Father's bedroom while he was shaving. 'Pop', I said, 'I've decided to give up dancing and go to college.' He replied without looking away from the mirror. 'I'm glad you have, my dear. I don't think you would have been happy.'"

The University of California at Los Angeles

After giving up on ballet, Agnes enrolled at the University of California at Los Angeles (UCLA; then known as UC-Southern Branch). The campus was only a short walk from her house, so she continued to live at home. She took her studies as seriously as she had taken her dancing. She often took more than the required course load and worked very hard. Though she was very happy at the university, she did not abandon dance entirely. During the beginning of her sophomore year a revue was being held to help victims of a fire. Agnes volunteered to dance. This was the first time she ever danced on a stage. Occasionally she also staged dances for student events.

In her junior year, Agnes presented a skit that linked jazz dancing to the sounds, rhythms, and images of the jungle. Her father was in the theater to see it. He was greatly impressed and told her he thought he might work it in to his next film. Agnes was thrilled, and began thinking about how to put it all together and present it to him. The next night at dinner, he told her he had given the idea to Kosloff and that Kosloff also agreed it was good. Agnes was stunned and terribly disappointed that her idea was passed on for someone else to bring to life. Her father must have sensed something was wrong. Things were tense around the house until he announced that he would not use the dance after all.

The Importance of Ballet

Most dancers and choreographers today will say that a strong dancer must have ballet training. Ballet is often considered the foundation of a dancer's technique. Most dance forms use vocabulary that comes from ballet. Those considering a career in dance would be wise to start taking ballet.

Seventeen-year-old Agnes de Mille (*reclining, foreground*) dances with a friend at the University of California, Los Angeles (UCLA). Before beginning at UCLA, de Mille had decided to give up formal dance lessons, but while there she created skits and dance pantomimes. After graduating from UCLA, de Mille tried with only limited success to find work as a choreographer and dancer, mostly in New York City and London, England.

Agnes continued dancing at various student rallies and began practicing regularly on her own again in her bedroom after finishing her studying. One day her younger sister, Margaret, had brought home a male actor friend named Douglass Montgomery, or Dug. Agnes was rehearsing in the living room, and he asked when she would next be performing. She invited him to her next performance, and he was greatly impressed. He said she was a great dancer and performer and that she should leave the university and go into the theater. This moment was a revelation for Agnes, who says in *Dance to the Piper*, "This boy simply said what I had waited all my life to hear." She and Dug formed a great friendship based on their shared love of theater, his for acting and hers for dancing. He thought she should move to New York City right away. Agnes decided to wait and finished her education, graduating cum laude (with honors) at the age of twenty in June 1926.

Shortly after graduation, Agnes learned her parents were divorcing. This upsetting event helped make up Agnes's mind. She and Margaret moved with their mother back to New York City. Robert Emmet Long, in *Broadway, the Golden Years*, describes the momentous developments that would come next: "So in the autumn of 1926, while living with her mother and sister in a duplex on West Sixty-seventh Street, just off Central Park, Agnes ventured out 'to change the American theatre.'"

3 The World Takes Notice

Agnes de Mille was not well prepared as she went out to seek dance work in New York City. Throughout her college years, she hadn't been regularly training. In addition, her specialty was ballet, but most of the available work was in the styles that were popular at that time, like tap choruses and line routines. In the meantime, de Mille began to choreograph her own dances. These she would share with her friend Dug, who by this time had also moved to New York to build his acting career. She also started to audition for agents.

However, de Mille was not getting offers from the agents. So, with the help of her mother, she went to Santa Fe, New Mexico, to give her own dance concert. Her ticket sales met her expenses, which to de Mille and her mother meant success. Her first real taste of success, however, came from a recital she shared with Jacques Cartier, a fellow

The world famous Radio City Rockettes appear on the stage of New York's Radio City Music Hall in 1937. Originally formed as the Missouri Rockets in 1925 in St. Louis, the company was brought to New York in 1932 by promoter S. L. "Roxy" Rothafel and renamed the Roxyettes before becoming the Rockettes. They soon perfected the chorus line—a popular American form of line dance that emphasizes precision and uniformity of movement.

dancer and choreographer. The performance sold out, and de Mille's dances were met with great applause. John Martin, a dance critic at that time, wrote in the *New York Times*: "Here is undoubtedly one of the brightest stars now rising above our native horizon" (as quoted in *Dance to the Piper*). With newfound confidence, de Mille resumed her auditions. But once again, these were met with disappointment. She was told again and again that she was meant for concert dance, not for the theater.

The Friendship and Influence of Martha Graham

In the summer of 1928, de Mille was a guest soloist with Adolph Bolm's company on his autumn tour. She was to perform three of her own pieces. Bolm had danced with Pavlova and had been a character dancer with Diaghilev's Ballets Russes in Paris. He now had his own ballet company that toured the United States. This tour brought de Mille into contact with Louis Horst. Horst wrote and arranged dance music and had been an accompanist to many concert dancers. He was very supportive of dancers and taught them how to use music to develop and structure dances. Horst was a collaborator with Martha Graham (a pioneer in modern dance), and he introduced de Mille to her.

Graham and de Mille became friends, and de Mille began exploring concert dance. She greatly respected Graham's opinions. Even though their dance styles were different, de Mille often went to Graham for help and advice. Traditionally, the goal of ballet was to conceal the dancer's effort. Graham, however, thought that effort was important; effort was, in her opinion, life itself. Graham used this

Agnes de Mille (*right*) appears with her good friend and fellow pioneering choreographer Martha Graham in 1974. De Mille is presenting Graham with the Edward MacDowell Medal, awarded every year to an American creative artist whose body of work has made an outstanding contribution to the national culture. This was the first time a MacDowell award had ever gone to someone working in the field of dance.

idea as inspiration for her choreography. During this time of friendship with Graham, de Mille worked on her own skills as a choreographer. As stated by Carol Easton in *No Inter-missions*, "She was trying to learn to compose dances that were not pantomimes, not dramatic stories, but planned sequences of sustained movement which would be original and compelling."

Europe

In 1929, de Mille was asked to choreograph and dance in a revival of *The Black Crook* (first produced in 1866 and said to be the first Broadway musical, *The Black Crook* was based on a play by Charles M. Barras). It was her first chance to choreograph for a group of dancers. This opportunity led to her meeting Warren Leonard, who became her dancing partner and friend for the next few years. Around this time, de Mille moved out of her mother's house and found her own apartment.

Leonard and de Mille were becoming desperate to find dance work. Finally, they were hired to choreograph a revue for producer Max Gordon. Though happy for the work, de Mille and Leonard soon felt like they were in over their heads. Rehearsals were difficult, and de Mille felt unprepared. This proved to be quite a learning experience for them. Unfortunately, de Mille and Leonard were replaced before the opening. After assessing her failure, de Mille decided to go to Europe.

In 1932, de Mille moved to London, England, where she trained with Marie Rambert's Ballet Club (which later became Ballet Rambert). Rambert was a tough teacher who had studied with Émile Jaques-Dalcroze and Enrico Cecchetti. Under Rambert's guidance, de Mille learned a great deal and further developed her technique. Two other major choreographers, Antony Tudor and Frederick Ashton, also studied with and influenced de Mille. She became great friends with Tudor as well as the dancer Hugh Laing. Laing partnered de Mille in every concert she gave while she was in England.

For de Mille, the mid- to late 1930s were filled with frustration and setbacks. She was offered a number of opportunities to choreograph for various movies, but they all fell through for a number of reasons. At this time, as de Mille states in *Dance to the Piper*, she felt as though her family, ". . . all except mother, had given up hope of a brilliant career for [her]." Her mother always supported her, even in the worst of times. According to Anna de Mille herself, "I've always been proud of her. Always. When no one hired her" (as quoted in *Dance to the Piper*).

"Rodeo"

For a brief time in the early 1940s, de Mille toured with a small company of her own. It was during this time, through Martha Graham, that she met Walter Prude, a theatrical agent and an army officer who would later become her husband. Her dance concert career was also picking up. She had been invited to perform with the American Ballet Theatre.

During this time she choreographed her first full-length ballet, *Black Ritual* (1940). This ballet was the first to use black dancers. In 1942, she learned that the Ballet Russe de Monte Carlo, an offshoot of Diaghilev's

In 1942, Agnes de Mille choreographed "Rodeo," a ballet set in the American West, to music by Aaron Copland. She also served as the principal dancer in the role of the cowgirl, who takes a ranch job and dresses like a man in order to be closer to the head wrangler with whom she has fallen in love.

original company, was interested in performing new American work. De Mille jumped at this opportunity. Before she had left London she had choreographed a recital program, *American Suite*, which was made up of four dances, including one titled "Rodeo" (1942). This dance was based on a square dance she had attended in Colorado. The dance expressed different aspects of cowboy life, including pantomimes of cowboys riding horses at the rodeo. De Mille quickly created a story to go along with the dance and presented the idea to the Ballet Russe de Monte Carlo.

The Ballet Russe accepted the idea. Aaron Copland wrote the score, and de Mille danced the lead. *American Suite* premiered in New York at the Metropolitan Opera House on October 16, 1942. The program sold out opening night. In *Dance to the Piper*, de Mille admits, "This was not a great performance. We gave better, later. Neither was it a great ballet . . . But it was the first of its kind, and the moment was quick with birth." The audience loved it! The cast received twenty-two curtain calls.

This was the moment de Mille had been dreaming of and hoping for since she was a child. It represented a momentous turning point for her and her work: "If it is possible for a life to change at one given moment, if it is possible for all movement, growth and accumulated power to become apparent at one single point, then my hour struck at 9:40, October 16, 1942" (as quoted in *Dance to the Piper*). In *Broadway, the Golden Years*, Robert Emmet Long says that "Rodeo" "had a stunning freshness and distinctively American quality that made it a forerunner of other dance pieces with American settings and themes."

The next day, according to *OK! The Story of Oklahoma!*, de Mille received a telegram from Theresa Helburn, a producer with the Theatre Guild: "We think your work is enchanting. Come talk to us Monday."

Oklahoma!

In the early 1940s, famed lyricist Richard Rodgers

and composer Oscar Hammerstein II—collaborators still considered the masters of American musical theater—were putting together a musical version of *Green Grow the Lilacs*, which would later be known as *Oklahoma!* A play written by Lynn Riggs, *Green Grow the Lilacs* was based on frontier life in the Indian Territory of Oklahoma at the turn of the twentieth century. The success of "Rodeo" led Rodgers and Hammerstein to choose de Mille as their choreographer for *Oklahoma!* Dick Rodgers was a little concerned, however, that de Mille couldn't make the crossover from ballet to Broadway.

In *Green Grow the Lilacs*, Rodgers and Hammerstein wanted the choreography to be a major part of the story. The dances were designed to provide a great deal of information about the characters and the story. This was a new way of working. There was no real precedent for it. Rodgers and Hammerstein were a little worried. They questioned whether de Mille, who was inexperienced in theater, could be counted on to successfully tackle such a major and innovative task.

De Mille was well aware of Rodgers and Hammerstein's reservations. In *Dance to the Piper* she remarks, "Even after the success of 'Rodeo'

I just barely succeeded in getting the show." The deal was negotiated, and it was determined that she would receive 1,500 dollars for six weeks of work. Beyond that period, she would earn fifty dollars a week for ten weeks after the production costs of the show were paid.

Revolutionizing Broadway

This was de Mille's big chance. She had big ideas

Composer Richard Rodgers (*left*) and lyricist Oscar Hammerstein II collaborate on their show *Me and Juliet* in 1953. With Agnes de Mille, they produced one of the most popular and innovative shows in music theater history—1943's *Oklahoma!*

for the musical from the very beginning. She would introduce classical ballet steps to popular audiences by disguising them within the movements of the cowboy characters.

Unintimidated by her world-famous collaborators, de Mille was very vocal about her concerns. She disagreed with Rodgers and Hammerstein on casting the dancers. She insisted on pure dancing talent, while the directors were equally interested in matching the dancers' appearance to their characters. She also questioned the dance number that would end act 1 and persuaded them to put in another ballet instead. It was this ballet that would ultimately produce the most excitement among audiences and critics alike and influence many choreographers

Rodgers and Hammerstein

Rodgers and Hammerstein are one of the best-known teams in musical theater. Though they had known each other for many years, *Oklahoma!* was the first musical they wrote together. Following the huge success of *Oklahoma!*, they wrote the music and lyrics for numerous other successful musicals like *Carousel, The King and I, State Fair, South Pacific,* and *The Sound of Music.*

who came after de Mille. But, as stated in *Broadway, the Golden Years*, "it was the eighteen-minute dream ballet, 'Laurey Makes up Her Mind,' that left audiences stunned and lifted *Oklahoma!* into greatness . . . The influence of Agnes's dream ballet was phenomenal; for years it was as if every self-respecting musical had to have a dream ballet, until at last, through endless repetition, the vogue wore itself out."

Oklahoma! was a huge success. According to *Broadway, the Golden Years*, "No musical appearing on Broadway has ever had more historic significance . . . It transformed Agnes for a time into the most famous and talked about theatre choreographer in the world, and made dance a vital force in the musical." This musical set the tone for the "musical play" in which music, story, and dance were interwoven and important to the story. Thanks to Agnes de Mille and her ingenious innovation, American musical theater was changed forever.

4 De Mille's Lasting Legacy

Shortly after the success of *Oklahoma!*, de Mille returned to California for her wedding. She married Walter Prude in Beverly Hills on June 14, 1943. It was a very small and simple wedding with only nine guests in attendance. Prude was an officer in the military. Shortly after the wedding, he was sent overseas, while de Mille returned to New York to enjoy her recent success.

A String of Successes

Agnes de Mille became one of the most sought-after choreographers in America. She went on to choreograph numerous Broadway shows including *One Touch of Venus* (1943), *Bloomer Girl* (1944), and *Carousel* (1945). *Carousel* opened on Broadway on April 19, 1945. At that time, de Mille had four hit musicals running on Broadway at the same time. This greatly increased demand for her services in the entertainment industry and gave her greater freedom and power to choose her projects. As she explains in *Dance to the Piper*, "So now that financially and popularly speaking I was at the crest, I had first refusal of every script on Broadway, and although I had never been to Hollywood [for work], the offers reached unprecedented heights."

Her next big success following *Carousel* was *Brigadoon* (1947). The setting for *Brigadoon* is an enchanted village in the Scottish Highlands that emerges from the mists of time for one day every hundred years. To prepare for choreographing the dances, de Mille studied Scottish Highlands culture and the styles of Scottish dance. She also studied with many Scottish dancers in New York. She was very proud of her work on that show, and she considered those dances some of her best work to date. After *Brigadoon* opened, critic John Mason Brown remarked that de Mille had "mastered a new language," creating dances that were "among the finest to have been seen on an American stage" (as quoted in *Broadway, the Golden Years*).

However, the excitement didn't end there; de Mille discovered she was having a baby. Easton records de Mille's thoughts in *No Intermissions*: "'I wanted it all. I wanted

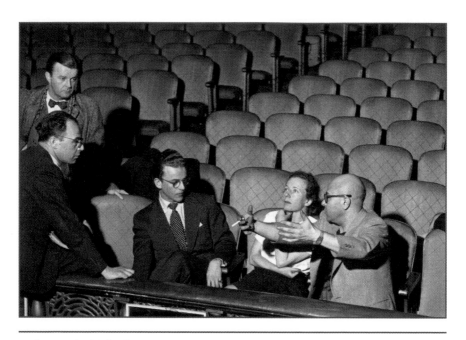

Agnes de Mille (*second from right*) and lyricist Alan Jay Lerner (*third from left*) talk during rehearsals for *Brigadoon* in 1947, made with Lerner's longtime composing partner Frederick Loewe. De Mille won one of her two Tony Awards for her Scottish-flavored choreography for this show.

wifehood, motherhood, and creativity in art . . . I felt capable of encompassing all.'" Jonathan de Mille Prude was born on April 20, 1946.

During the next year, de Mille went to work on a new Rodgers and Hammerstein musical, *Allegro* (1947). *Allegro* was an original story by Hammerstein, and de Mille was hired as choreographer and director. As de Mille explains in *Dance to the*

Piper, "This was a tremendous honor . . . As far as I knew, it was the first time a woman had been put in charge of a big Broadway musical. It was the first time, certainly, I had been offered a major show to direct."

Allegro opened on October 31, 1947. It received positive reviews, but those involved were somewhat disappointed in the outcome. It had been a difficult show to put together. The lighting and set designs, though creative, were difficult to work around. Rehearsals had to be in three separate locations, so de Mille was forced to run all over the city in her effort to direct the show. Three weeks before the opening, de Mille stepped down as director and began to focus only on the choreography, while Hammerstein staged the dramatic scenes and Rodgers wrote the songs. She still received credit as both choreographer and director, however, and this paved the way for future choreographer-directors to perform double duty. This was the last stage musical she would work on with Rodgers and Hammerstein.

Shortly after *Allegro*, de Mille choreographed her most famous ballet, *Fall River Legend* (1948). This ballet was about Lizzie Borden, who, in 1892, was widely believed to have murdered her parents in the New England town of Fall

Agnes de Mille (*second from left*) supervises a rehearsal of the Agnes de Mille Dance Theatre in 1953, the year the company was founded.

and *The Girl in Pink Tights* (1954). She also formed her own company, the Agnes de Mille Dance Theatre. Beginning in October 1953, the company went on tour to 126 cities. In 1955, de Mille went to Hollywood to choreograph a movie version of *Oklahoma!* However, a certain amount of tension arose when de Mille began working again with Rodgers and Hammerstein. Unlike her uncle and father, de Mille never found great success in Hollywood.

River. The ballet premiered at the Metropolitan Opera House on April 22, 1948. Many critics consider *Fall River Legend* to be de Mille's best ballet.

Afterward, de Mille continued to choreograph and direct for many more shows, including *Gentlemen Prefer Blondes* (1949), *Paint Your Wagon* (1951),

As de Mille's Broadway career slowed down, she

started writing and went on to become a successful author. Over the course of thirty years, she wrote more than a dozen books, including five memoirs. These books continued to add to her fame. *Dance to the Piper* (1952) was the first of these memoirs. It tells the story of her family background, her childhood years, her struggles making her way in the world of theater and dance, and her artistic and professional

The 1955 film poster for *Oklahoma!* appears above. Agnes de Mille had achieved such attention and fame for her Broadway choreography that her name appears prominently on the poster, just below those of Rodgers and Hammerstein. Despite the film's lavishness and popular success, de Mille was never fond of it and greatly preferred the stage version.

breakthrough with *Oklahoma!* A few years later, she wrote *And Promenade Home* (1958). This book describes her work on various early successful shows through *Carousel*. It also tells the story of her courtship with and marriage to Walter Prude. Some of her other books include *Speak to Me, Dance with Me* (1973), *Where the Wings Grow* (1978), *America Dances* (1981), and *Portrait Gallery* (1990). Her writing led her to another career as a highly paid lecturer. She gave lectures all over the country on dance and dance-related issues. From 1973 to 1974, de Mille founded and toured with the Agnes de Mille Heritage Dance Theater.

De Mille Makes Her Comeback

On May 15, 1975, while de Mille was preparing for a lecture and dance concert in the auditorium of the Hunter College Playhouse in New York City, she had a stroke that paralyzed her right side and almost killed her. De Mille survived, and with enormous determination, she trained herself to write with her left hand and began writing again.

Agnes de Mille's return to public life happened around the same time as the celebration of the bicentennial of the United States in 1976. This yearlong birthday party for the nation created renewed interest in de Mille's dances with their

American themes and settings. Ballet companies began presenting revivals of her work. American Ballet Theatre arranged a gala devoted to two of de Mille's most famous works, "Rodeo" and *Fall River Legend*. A letter from President Gerald Ford that praised de Mille for her uniquely American contribution to dance was read during the gala on July 8,

A frail and elderly Agnes de Mille is escorted by marine and navy servicemen back to her seat after accepting the National Medal of Arts from President Ronald Reagan (seen in the background) in 1986. Though hampered by the effects of a stroke, de Mille continued to work, creating two final ballets, *The Informer* (1988) and *The Other* (1992), for the American Ballet Theatre.

Praise from a Dance Legend

In *Dance to the Piper,* de Mille shares a conversation she had with Martha Graham. De Mille was complaining about her lack of technique, to which Graham replied, "Technique! I can see technique at Radio City. From you I ask something greater than that . . . what cannot be learned in any class . . . Your American studies have given me courage."

1976. In addition, New York City mayor Abraham Beame presented her with the Handel Medallion, the city's highest award for artistic achievement.

In the following years, de Mille went on to receive great recognition for her achievements and garnered many more awards. In 1979, de Mille attended a White House dinner given in her honor by President Jimmy Carter. In 1980, she received the Kennedy Center Career Achievement Award, and in 1986, de Mille was awarded the National Medal of Arts at the White House by President Ronald Reagan. Throughout the 1980s, de Mille became known to the public as the premier choreographer of American theatrical dance.

A Dance Original

Agnes de Mille was a true originator in the dance world. She worked hard and was determined to be a part

Agnes de Mille is honored in this American Choreographers commemorative stamp series released by the U.S. Post Office in 2004.

of something big. In her autobiography *Dance to the Piper*, de Mille describes how it felt to be dancing in a time of such creative energy, when she had the opportunity to meet and work with other dance pioneers such as Martha Graham, Doris Humphrey, and Frederick Ashton: "We risked everything. Every one of us had thrown overboard all our traditions . . . and were out to remodel our entire craft. No one helped us and there were no rules. We worked alone. We struck sparks from one another. I am glad I participated in the period of the originators. There is a force and wonder in first revelation that has no duplicate."

On October 7, 1993, de Mille died in her home in New York City at the age of eighty-eight. From the time she was a child until her death, dance was her passion. It has been said by some that it was her obsession. As Robert Emmet Long says in *Broadway, the Golden Years*, "She won some great battles and took enormous losses, but she never lost her awesome will to leave her mark on her time."

Glossary

choreographer-director A person who creates and designs dances as well as directs the acting in a show.

concert dance Dance that is presented as its own art form.

curtain call An appearance by a performer to take his or her bows in response to the applause of the audience, after the end of a theatrical production.

improvisation To compose, write, dance, or sing without preplanning or rehearsing.

marquee A large sign, often lit, above a theater announcing the show and credits.

musical theater A genre of theatrical production that uses singing, dancing, and acting to tell the story.

pantomime To tell a story silently, using only body actions and facial movements; often used in drama and dance.

revival A version of a play or dance staged years after the original version was first produced and presented.

revue A theatrical production that features skits, songs, and dances.

score The music for a movie or theatrical production.

For More Information

Broadway Dance Center
221 West 57th Street, 5th floor
New York, NY 10019
(212) 582-9304
Web site: http://www.broadwaydancecenter.com

Dance Films Association
48 West 21st Street #907
New York, NY 10010
(212) 727-0764
Web site: http://www.dancefilmsassn.org

Web Sites

Due to the changing nature of Internet links, the Rosen Publishing Group, Inc., has developed an online list of Web sites related to the subject of this book. This site is updated regularly. Please use this link to access the list:

http://www.rosenlinks.com/lac/agde

For Further Reading

Derezinski, Amelia. *Star Turns: Dancing on Broadway*. New York, NY: The Rosen Publishing Group, 2004.

Green, Kay, and Stanley Green. *Broadway Musicals Show by Show*. 5th ed. Milwaukee, WI: Hal Leonard Publishing Corporation, 1997.

Bibliography

De Mille, Agnes. *Dance to the Piper: Memoirs of the Ballet*. Boston, MA: Little, Brown and Company, 1958.

De Mille, Agnes. *And Promenade Home*. Boston: Little, Brown and Company, 1958.

Easton, Carol. *No Intermissions: The Life of Agnes de Mille*. Boston, MA: Little, Brown and Company, 1996.

Long, Robert Emmet. *Broadway, the Golden Years: Jerome Robbins and the Great Choreographer-Directors, 1940 to the Present*. New York, NY: Continuum International Publishing Group Inc., 2001.

Wilk, Max. *OK! The Story of Oklahoma! A Celebration of America's Most Loved Musical*. New York, NY: Applause, 2002.

Index

A

Agnes de Mille Dance
    Theater, 38
Agnes de Mille Heritage
    Dance Theater, 40
Allegro, 36–37
American Ballet Theatre,
    27, 41
American Suite, 28–29
Ashton, Frederick, 26, 43

B

Ballet Russe de Monte
    Carlo, 27–28
Ballets Russes, 14, 24, 27
Black Crook, The, 25
Black Ritual, 27
Bloomer Girl, 34
Bolm, Adolph, 24
Brigadoon, 35

C

Carousel, 32, 34, 35, 40
Cartier, Jacques, 22–23
Cecchetti, Enrico, 26
Copland, Aaron, 28

D

Dance to the Piper, 4,
    6–7, 8, 14–15, 17, 18,
    21, 23, 27, 29, 30, 35,
    36–37, 39–40, 42, 43
de Mille, Agnes
    awards given to, 42
    books written by, 39–40
    childhood and education
        of, 6–13, 14–21

shows choreographed
    by, 25–26, 27–33,
    34–35, 36–38
de Mille, Anna (mother),
    4, 6, 7, 10, 11, 12,
    13, 17, 21, 22, 26, 27
De Mille, Cecil B. (uncle),
    7–8, 10, 14, 38
de Mille, Margaret (sister),
    6, 10, 13, 14, 20, 21
de Mille, William (father),
    6, 8, 10, 12, 17–18,
    19, 38
Diaghilev, Sergei, 14, 24,
    27–28
Duncan, Isadora, 11

F

Fall River Legend,
    37–38, 41

G

Goldfish (Goldwyn),
    Sam, 8
Gordon, Max, 26
Graham, Martha, 24–25,
    27, 42, 43

H

Hammerstein, Oscar,
    29–30, 32, 36, 37, 38
Helburn, Theresa, 29
Horst, Louis, 24
Humphrey, Doris, 43

J

Jaques-Dalcroze, Émile, 26

K
Kosloff, Theodore, 14–15, 19

L
Laing, Hugh, 26–27
Lasky, Jesse, 8
Leonard, Warren, 26

O
Oklahoma!, 4, 30–33, 34, 38, 40
One Touch of Venus, 34

P
Paramount Pictures (Lasky
    Company), 8

Pavlova, Anna, 11, 12, 24
Prude, Walter, 27, 34, 40

R
Rambert, Marie, 26
Rodgers, Richard, 29–30, 32, 36,
    37, 38

S
St. Denis, Ruth, 11

T
Tudor, Antony, 26

About the Author

Originally from Maine, Rachel Gaskill is a dancer, choreographer, and teacher. She has taught for numerous dance organizations, public and private schools, and studios. She currently resides in New Jersey with her husband.

Photo Credits

Cover background, cover foreground, pp. 1, 13, 16, 23, 25, 31 © Bettmann/Corbis; pp. 5, 39 © 20th Century Fox/Everett Collection; pp. 7, 11, 20, 36, 38 © Jerome Robbins Dance Division, The New York Public Library for the Performing Arts, Astor, Lenox, and Tilden Foundations; p. 9 © The DeMille Estate; p. 28 photograph by Maurice Seymour, courtesy of Ronald Seymour; p. 41 © Diana Walker/Time Life Pictures/Getty Images; p. 43 © United States Postal Service.

Designer: Tahara Anderson
Developmental Editor: Nancy Allison, CMA, RME